Lost and Found

A Guide to the LAP-BAND® Journey

By Dr. Nirmal Jayaseelan and Cynthia Jones O'Kelly

Printed at Slocum Printing, Inc. - Dallas
Written and edited by Kim Pierce
Designed by Ric Martin
Speical thanks to our cover models:
 Betti Coffey and Lisa Knowles

Acknowledgments

This book is the culmination of a lot of hard work – and a total labor of love. But we could not have done it without the unwavering support and encouragement of so many friends, family members, professional associates and patients.

We are both grateful to our colleagues in the gastric-banding community – surgeons, co-workers and fellow banded folks. It is a pleasure to work with each and every one as we continue on this evolving journey.

We want to thank Paige McDaniel for reading the first draft, giving great bandster comments and testing each of the recipes.

We are grateful to Kim Pierce and Ric Martin. Without their know-how, this book would not make sense nor would it have been completed.

And we are indebted to the patients who agreed to participate in this book. Their stories are awesome and inspiring. Because they had the courage to share their experiences, readers everywhere will find the courage to change their lives, too.

I would especially like to thank my wife, Preethi, for being a wonderful mother and creating a loving and nurturing home. I also thank my children – Zubin, Meera and Kirin – for being so patient. And finally, I am grateful to my parents, Sam and Katherine Jayaseelan, for whose love, discipline and sacrifice I am forever indebted.

– Dr. Nirmal Jayaseelan

I want to thank my husband, Nick, who is my knight in shining armor, and his children who are now my children, Edward, Julia, Jack, Brendan and Martha. I would also like to thank my mother, Phyllis Jones; my sister, Martha Hooper, and her husband Dan and their children, Jack and Kate; as well as my brother, Stuart Jones, and his girlfriend, Holly Zimmerman.

I would have to single out my sister, Martha, who had the courage to tell me about the LAP-BAND®, which started me on the road to a new life. I would also like to thank Vern Vincent for his part in creating such a magnificent device!

– Cynthia Jones O'Kelly

Lost and Found

A Guide to the LAP-BAND® Journey

Contents

Introduction | Why This Book is Important to Us

We got together to write this book because we wanted to provide a simple, easy-to-read guide that explains and demystifies LAP-BAND® weight-loss surgery. We also wanted to create a complete guide that covers not only the technical aspects of LAP-BAND® surgery from A to Z, but also explains what happens inside your head when you become banded and start losing weight. Again and again we see that for most people, the journey isn't just about shedding pounds: It's also about reclaiming the person who's been buried inside. Hence, the title: *Lost and Found: A Guide to the LAP-BAND® Journey*.

We are also passionate about writing this because we believe the LAP-BAND® System changes lives. We've seen it, and we've lived it. One of us is a patient advocate who has had the LAP-BAND® surgery. The other is among the most experienced LAP-BAND® surgeons in the world, having performed more than 3,000 LAP-BAND® procedures.

We believe that if you're a heavy person who has tried diets and failed, someone who's weight has made them miserable, someone who's fed up with the limitations – not to mention the health risks – that go along with being overweight or obese, this book will change your life.

When we started writing it, we worked together in the same bariatric medical practice: surgeon and patient advocate. Here's what each of us has to say individually about why we're writing this:

The surgeon, Dr. Nirmal Jayaseelan
(pronounced jay-uh-SEE-lan)

I'm a general surgeon, but I perform LAP-BAND® and related surgery almost exclusively now. I've been at Medical City Dallas Hospital since 1999, and Medical City has been in bariatrics for at least 25 years.

Most surgeons, when they get out of medical school, have to do a lot of emergency-room work to build their practices. In general surgery,

Now, my waiting room is almost like a party. It's filled with joy and hope instead of fear and doubt. Daily, I see how this surgery changes people's lives. That makes the surgery very rewarding as a practice. But there has always been one piece missing: a resource that tells people what they need to know to decide if the surgery is right for them.

you deal with a lot of chronic disease: diabetics having limbs removed, breast cancer, colon cancer. The waiting room is a quiet, solemn place for these patients.

Several years ago, I started assisting in bariatric procedures. I thought that this would become only a part of my practice.

I really like long-term relationships with people, which is important with this type of surgery. One recommendation led to another, and that part of my practice just grew.

Now, my waiting room is almost like a party. It's filled with joy and hope instead of fear and doubt. Daily, I see how this surgery changes people's lives. That makes the surgery very rewarding as a practice.

But there has always been one piece missing: a resource that tells people what they need to know to decide if the surgery is right for them. My job in this book is to provide the medical information you need to make that decision and what you need to know for your weight loss to be successful.

The patient advocate, Cynthia Jones O'Kelly

I've been banded for almost 10 years. I got the LAP-BAND® in 1999 before it was approved for use in the United States when I was a subject in the second round of U.S. Food and Drug Administration safety trials in New Orleans. Then Dr. J replaced that band with the current model in 2005.

Before getting banded, I spent 29 years being overweight, obese, and ultimately miserable. By the time I was 36, I weighed 340 pounds, and I'm 5-feet-1-inch tall. After two years with the band, I reached 140, a weight I've maintained since with the typical ups and downs.

I became a patient advocate because, when I went through the dramatic weight loss, there was no one to tell me what was happening beyond the clinical, medical changes. There was no one to explain the emotional issues that would come up as the pounds melted away, nor to offer a clue about rebuilding a social life after so many years of isolation. (I am pleased to report that I not only conquered dating, but am happily married!)

For me, providing insight into what happens in your head and heart, as well as helping others with after-care support, became an obsession. And as it turns out, studies suggest that this ongoing care is a necessary part of the success formula. I started an independent after-care group, then teamed with Dr. J in his practice and am now a Program Director for Medical Edge Healthcare Group, Inc.

I want this book to become the LAP-BAND® bible, so that bandsters everywhere will have the tools and support they need to navigate banding successfully. If this piques your curiosity, turn to Chapter 1, where I tell my story in depth.

Cynthia: A dream come true

Before my LAP-BAND® procedure

After my LAP-BAND® procedure

Chapter 1 | Introduction to the LAP-BAND®

If you think we cannot possibly know how you feel right now, holding this book in your hand and contemplating surgery after more failed diets than you care to count, more embarrassing moments than you want to remember, and maybe even the sense that nothing, not even this, is ever going to work for you, just wait. We want to tell a story.

The year was 1999. *I was 36. I weighed 340 pounds on a 5-foot-1-inch frame. I had tried every diet in the world, and I still was desperately overweight. I couldn't walk up stairs without huffing and puffing. I couldn't attract a man. I'd never had a real boyfriend. I couldn't please my parents. And it was dawning on me that this was all there was ever going to be for me. I wasn't going to have the husband, the Suburban, the house, the kids. I was stuck, and life wasn't going to get any better.*

The reality hit me hard one particular night. I was in my bedroom. I dropped to my knees and raised my fist to God. "This is it," I said. I don't normally kneel when I pray. But this time, I did – next to my bed after climbing the stairs and breaking into a sweat.

I pounded my fists on the bed. I yelled at God:

"What did I do to deserve this, God? What did I do? I've tried to be a good person. I've tried to do the right thing. And when I've made mistakes, I've tried to learn from them and become a better person. Why don't I deserve to be happy? Why don't I deserve to fall in love and get married? Where is my knight in shining armor? Heck, I don't even have a knight in rusty armor."

The strain of my weight was too great to stay on my knees, and I fell back on my butt. Sitting in the floor, I lashed out again as tears of frustration squeezed from my eyes. I was furious.

And I was sad.

"You must want me to be this way," I said. Not out of self-pity, but in a twisted kind of surrender. "You must want my health to be screwed up. You must want me never to have a kid. You must want me never to have the things I've longed for

What is the LAP-BAND®?

The LAP-BAND® System was the first adjustable gastric band to be approved for use in the United States. Gastric banding is the least invasive, safest form of surgical weight-loss available in this country for severely overweight and obese people. It is adjustable, and the surgery is reversible. The LAP-BAND® itself is a hollow Silastic ring that fits around the top of your stomach and is connected by thin tubing to a port that's attached just below the skin.

and worked so hard for in my life."

I am a Presbyterian. I believe in predestination. I believe that God has a plan for everything. But at that moment, I was thinking: "This is His plan for me? How screwed up is that?"

And so I said: "I give up. You win. I'll just go ahead and exist this way and die early because that's clearly what you've laid out for me."

How can I explain the grim acceptance that followed this surrender prayer? It was like the huge sigh when you finally give up.

But it wasn't a happy sigh. It was a sigh of resignation. Like a cancer patient near death. An animal overtaken by its attackers. Someone who's lost the only person they've ever loved.

The pain and the anger were still there, without relief. No weight had been lifted. I was still going to go to bed fat and wake up fat the next morning.

But if this was what God wanted for me, so be it. I wasn't going to fight it any longer. Whatever hopes and dreams I had were effectively snuffed out with that prayer. Thy will be done.

I told no one about this. And I believed, for whatever reason, that I must deserve this fate. One week later, I got the phone call that changed my life.

It led me to become one of the first recipients of the then-experimental adjustable gastric band. I was a subject in the second U.S. Food and Drug Administration trials. Just look at my photo as a radiant bride to see what that surgery has meant to me.

Over the two years after I was banded, I lost over 200 pounds. And I have kept it off, with minor ups an d downs, ever since.

Not only that, I recently celebrated the third anniversary of my marriage to the most wonderful man I know, and he came with a ready-made family of five children! I am so passionate about sharing my experience and giving hope to people like me that I have dedicated my professional life to assisting others through the gastric-banding process.

When I tell people about my experience, they say, "Cynthia, you lost a whole person."

And I say back, "No, I found one."

If you're thinking this could never happen to you and it must be a special case – like those weight-loss ads with the asterisk and the fine print that says, "results not typical" – we're here to tell you that these results *are* well within the norm.

When you read the stories in this book and look at the before-and-after pictures we've included, you'll see that these people are a lot like you. They are men and women who felt desperate and hopeless about their weight and who turned to surgery as a last resort.

They weren't looking to become bikini models. They just wanted to lose enough weight to reclaim their health and lives.

Now, let us tell you something about the adjustable gastric band, what it is and how it works, so you can decide whether you want to start your own journey.

Introduction to the LAP-BAND®

First, a little background on how your stomach works: Your stomach is like a butter churn that churns and breaks up food. It has two valves, one on top and one at the bottom.

When you eat a big meal, like Thanksgiving dinner, your stomach fills from the bottom up. You're sitting at

What is the band inflated with?
Sterile saline solution.

How does it work?
The LAP-BAND® fits around the top of your stomach, creating a small pouch. It helps you lose weight by restricting the amount of food you can eat at any one time and sending a message to the brain that you're full. The LAP-BAND® expands like an inner tube of a bicycle tire when saline solution is introduced by a doctor through the port. By filling or emptying the inner tube, you and your doctor can control the amount of restriction.

How much weight can I expect to lose?

Weight loss varies from patient to patient, and the amount you lose will depend on several factors. Obesity surgery is not a miracle cure, and the pounds won't come off by themselves. You will lose weight gradually. In fact, during the first four to six weeks after surgery while you are healing, you may not lose any weight at all.

You need to be prepared to commit to a new lifestyle and eating habits, and you will want to set realistic goals. *A weight loss of 2 to 3 pounds a week in the first year after the operation is possible. But 1 pound a week is more realistic.*

Twelve to eighteen months after your surgery, the rate of weight loss usually slows down. Your primary goal should be to achieve a weight loss that prevents, improves, or resolves health problems connected with severe obesity. Physical activity is another factor that can affect the speed of your weight loss.

the table. You're eating the turkey, the dressing, the gravy, the sweet potatoes. And by the time you get to the pumpkin pie with the whipped cream, the top of your stomach is stretched.

When the top of your stomach stretches, you get that certain feeling in the back of your throat when you have to lean back and loosen your belt. You are full. The top of the stomach is where the sensors are that send this "full!" message to your brain. Once that part of the stomach stretches, you're not interested in food anymore.

When the LAP-BAND® is put in place, it creates a new, smaller stomach pouch at the top of your stomach so that you feel full after eating less. After a meal, the contents of the pouch slowly empty through a small opening into your stomach, where they are digested normally.

Unlike some forms of weight-loss surgery, the LAP-BAND® doesn't involve stapling or rerouting, nor does it permanently change the shape of your stomach. It is usually day surgery, and it is easily reversible. The adjustable gastric band is the safest, least-invasive form of surgical weight loss available in the United States today.

The LAP-BAND® was the first adjustable gastric band approved by the FDA and the one we have used since its approval, which is why we refer to it specifically in this book. (Other types of bands, in addition to the LAP-BAND®, are in use in the United States and around the world.)

The LAP-BAND® itself is a hollow silicone ring that's placed around the upper part of the stomach to create the pouch. The band is connected to an access port by thin, kink-resistant silicone tubing. This port, which is anchored to the abdominal muscle just below the skin, allows the surgeon to adjust the size of the band to meet your individual weight-loss needs by adding or removing saline solution to inflate or deflate the band.

This directly impacts your appetite. Tightening the band makes you feel full and satisfied after eating much less food.

Most people with a normally tightened band lose between 1 and 3 pounds a week. That may not sound like a lot, but you don't want to lose weight too fast, the way people do with some forms of surgical weight-loss. Slow and steady gives your skin and body time to adjust to the new, shrinking you. Being adjustable is also an advantage of the band because everyone's stomach is a little different.

The LAP-BAND® is put in place laparoscopically through tiny abdominal incisions. In our experience, the operation usually takes about half an hour at an outpatient surgery center, although some surgeons do this operation in a hospital and require an overnight stay.

Working with an outpatient surgery

How much does the procedure cost? Where can I have it done?

Total costs for the LAP-BAND® surgical procedure are competitive across the country, and lower initial costs can be found outside the United States. There are also several methods for financing the procedure if your health-care provider does not pay for the surgery.

If you choose to have the surgery away from where you live, you will still need to locate a doctor in your area to handle your fills and follow-up care. Unlike other weight-loss surgeries, the LAP-BAND® works most effectively when you continue to see your surgeon three to four times a year. You will also be more successful if you participate in an after-care support network, which varies from practice to practice.

Is the surgery covered by insurance?

Many insurance companies now cover the LAP-BAND® procedure. However, even companies that routinely cover the surgery may have groups and individual policies that exclude coverage for the treatment of morbid obesity. You will need to check with your insurance provider to see if yours has such an exclusion. If you should be denied coverage, there is usually an appeal process. You will want to address the specific reason for the denial and provide supporting documentation. Specifically, you can appeal if your denial is based on one of the following reasons:

- *The LAP-BAND® System is investigational.*
- *The LAP-BAND® System is experimental.*
- *No knowledge of the LAP-BAND® System.*
- *Did not meet the criteria for surgery.*

center, you'll typically go home the same day. If you have to, you can have your surgery on a Friday and go back to work the following Monday, although it's better to take a few additional days off. After your stomach has healed from the surgery, usually about six weeks, the surgeon will schedule your first "fill," in which the band is inflated with saline solution.

You'll go in for four or six fills the first year, and the number after that will depend on how your weight loss is progressing. That brings us to another important difference between banding and other forms of weight-loss surgery.

Your relationship with your surgeon will continue after your surgery to ensure that the band is properly adjusted and that you are getting all the support and guidance you need to lose weight at a steady pace and make your weight-loss permanent. This post-surgery relationship is crucial to the success of your weight loss.

Having said all this, it's important to understand that the LAP-BAND® isn't a magic bullet. It does about 70 percent of the work by limiting how much you can eat. But it's up to you to do the other 30 percent. You'll have to ask yourself if you're ready to make and keep a commitment to eating and living differently.

The big difference between this and dieting is that the band will help you keep that commitment. It's a partnership. And we emphasize: **This is not a diet**. No one is going to send you home with a list of forbidden foods. You can eat anything you want. Anything. You just won't feel like eating as much.

You'll learn to make good food choices because you'll be eating less and needing to think more about getting enough of the right foods. For instance, we ask you to eat at least 60 grams of protein a day with the band so that you won't get too hungry between meals. To do that, you'll to have start thinking about how to get some protein at each meal.

But the beauty of this book is that we're going show you the best, easiest ways to do this. Think of *Lost and Found: A Guide to the LAP-BAND® Journey* as an insider's road map to living most effectively and successfully with the band.

Does this all sound too good to be true? Rest assured, it is not. There are already hundreds of thousands of people worldwide walking around with new lives they never dared imagine.

Will the LAP-BAND® System be as life-changing for you? Yes, without a doubt. We can't predict exactly what losing 50, 100 or even 150-plus pounds will mean to you, but we can assure you that your life will be different.

And the changes are likely to be quite dramatic. Here are some of the major differences we've seen over the past several years with patients:

• **Improved physical health.** We see blood pressure readings come down, healthier

Is my eligibility affected if I'm allergic to any medications?

Generally, being allergic to medicine will not prevent you from qualifying for surgery. But it's important for your doctor to know about any allergies.

Will I feel hungry or deprived with the LAP-BAND®?

If you follow the nutrition guidelines when you choose food and then chew it well, you should not feel hungry or deprived. The LAP-BAND® makes you eat less in two ways: First, it reduces the capacity of your stomach. Second, it increases the amount of time it takes food to travel through your digestive system. You should feel full after eating a smaller meal than you are used to.

After surgery, can I eat anything I want in moderation?

After your stomach has healed, you may eat most foods. However, because you can eat only a little at a time, it becomes important to include foods that are good sources of vitamins and nutrients. If you eat foods that contain lots of sugar and fat, such as milkshakes, or drink liquids full of empty calories, such as juice beverages, the effectiveness of the LAP-BAND® will be greatly reduced or even cancelled.

blood sugar levels, and freer and easier breathing. As the weight comes off, patients report increased energy, fewer body aches and pains, and sounder sleep. In some cases, they are able to decrease or eliminate medications, with their doctor's approval.

• **Improved psychological health.** Patients say they feel better about themselves. Their self-esteem improves, and they feel less depressed. They exude more confidence, their social skills improve, and they express realistic hopes about the future.

• **Relationship change.** The LAP-BAND® will produce changes in your relationships with friends, family and co-workers, as well as in your love relationships.

In general, these changes are positive and exciting. They are also demanding.

Patients have to learn to put their own health-care choices first. This is often a change, since many people who are overweight or obese feel depressed and hopeless, and give their own lives the lowest priority.

Patients have to learn to make assertive, healthy decisions for themselves, even when those decisions upset loved ones. For instance, they may choose to go on their exercise walk instead of going to Starbucks for a Frappuccino with a friend. Or they may have to deal with their spouse's jealousy or discomfort when they become increasingly attractive and self-confident.

• **Improved body image.** Patients undergo incredible changes in how they see their bodies and how they feel about their bodies. Dramatic weight-loss creates drastic changes in size, appearance, and related areas such as clothing possibilities and feelings of attractiveness.

Just think about being able to walk into a store and buy clothes off the rack. Or getting onto an airplane and not having to request a seatbelt extension. Learning to accept a normal body image is sometimes a major challenge for obesity surgery patients. Sometimes they will still feel fat despite being a fraction of their former size.

It's also common to worry that you will gain the weight back. But we find that, as more time passes, patients become experts in managing their lives. As they experience real success, their new, healthier body-images become more comfortable and acceptable. And remember, success with the LAP-BAND® is the rule, not the exception.

Are you ready to learn more? We'll start by looking at some common weight-loss strategies and why they don't work, beginning with the story an actor whose voice you might recognize as Principal Moss from *King of the Hill.*

Dennis: Playing against type

Before my LAP-BAND® procedure

After my LAP-BAND® procedure

Retired actor Dennis Burkley knows how it feels to go on a diet and fail because, like so many people who chose the become banded, he tried and failed at more diets than he cares to count. "I had gotten so big," Dennis says from his home in Los Angeles, "and I tried every diet. Every time, if I lost, I would always gain back more than I lost."

Still, for a long time, Dennis was lucky. Even at his heaviest, tipping the scales at 360 pounds on a 6-foot-3-inch frame, he'd managed to dodge most of the health problems that come with obesity. Until his mid-50s.

Ironically, his weight had helped him get jobs as a film and TV actor: "I was the big, hairy biker guy," he says. You might remember him as Cal in Sanford, *Dozer in* Mask *or Butcher in* An Innocent Man *in addition to a blizzard of smaller roles. He was also Principal Moss and other voices on* King of the Hill.

But Dennis eventually developed diabetes and high blood pressure, which drove him to investigate the LAP-BAND®. "I wanted to drop 100 pounds," he says, noting that in his case health, not size, was the big motivator. He did research on the different kinds of gastric weight-loss surgery and concluded that the LAP-BAND® was safest.

"The hardest part for me was the week fasting before, and the week after the surgery," he says. Both the pre-op and post-op diets are strict, but important for medical reasons we'll explain in a moment.

"It was very hard. I was drinking as much bouillon as I could get. The truth of the matter is, I think I lost 17 pounds before surgery just from not eating anything." And he had a smooth recovery: "The beauty of my surgery was, the next day I was up and walked 30 minutes around the park."

Dennis got his LAP-BAND® in late 2005. Today, he has lost his 100 pounds and then some. One of the ways he facilitated weight loss was by working out extra hard at the gym. And while activity is a part of the LAP-BAND® weight-loss formula, not everyone chooses to do it the way he did. "I work out because I feel better when I work out. I worked out harder because I wanted to have a muscular body."

The LAP-BAND®

Today, he feels good at 230, and one of the things he likes most about his new, streamlined body is being able to shop for clothes off the rack at regular stores. "All my life, I've had to go to a big man's store. Now, I can just go to any store. I can go to the Gap. And I can dress nicer and look better in my clothes."

Most important to Dennis, though, has been the dramatic improvement in his health. "Since I've had the LAP-BAND®, I'm still on insulin, but it's down from 150 units a day to 40. I still take blood pressure medicine, but it's under control." He adds: "I wouldn't want to weigh less. I look skinny now."

How many times and how many ways have you tried to lose weight? Have you counted calories? Counted carbs? Done the grapefruit diet? The South Beach Diet? Have you exercised and struggled to lose pounds, only to watch them come back with a vengeance?

While it's true that diet and exercise, and some weight-loss programs, such as Weight Watchers and Jenny Craig, do help you lose weight, the odds are stacked against your keeping it off. Research suggests that without surgery the weight will come back. For most people, diet and exercise aren't the answer, and it's not because you're lazy.

Scientists are increasingly coming to believe that heredity is destiny and that powerful biological forces work to maintain the body's weight within a fixed, predetermined range. Our bodies are also better adapted to hoarding calories than losing them.

Celebrities who have their own trainers and chefs and who are paid to look good can be successful with diet and exercise because they've got a legion of people to keep them on track. But even Oprah Winfrey has watched the pounds creep back and has given up her struggle to remain a size 10, vowing not to diet again.

Scientific research is confirming that obesity has a powerful genetic link. And once you become obese, willpower has very little to do with changing it – any more than you'd expect a diabetic like Dennis to use will power to control his blood sugar.

At one time in human history – in fact,

What are the advantages of the LAP-BAND®?

- *The LAP-BAND® involves minimally invasive surgery that is usually performed at an outpatient surgical center. It is typically put in place through several tiny incisions in the abdomen.*
- *Your stomach remains intact: There's no cutting or stapling of your stomach.*
- *Your digestive tract is not rerouted.*
- *The digestive process remains the same: The food you eat still passes through the lower stomach and the full length of the intestine. This is different from bypass surgery, which uses a part of the intestine to literally bypass the stomach.*
- *Nutrients are fully absorbed the same as before banding.*
- *You do not experience dumping syndrome, which is an uncomfortable reaction to sugar in the initial years after bypass surgery.*
- *The band is adjustable. It increases satiety and encourages you to gradually eat less. It can also be loosened to let more food flow through, something you would want if you became pregnant, for example.*

for most of human history – the ability to effectively store and hold onto fat appears to have been an evolutionary advantage. Throughout time, a body's ability to hoard fat in times of plenty increased the chances of survival during the periodic famines that would arise.

But today, we're surrounded by plenty, and the famine never comes. Our bodies, highly skilled at storing energy, will fight to hold onto it.

Some bodies are better at this than others, marshaling enzymes to carry out the task. One example of an enzyme that affects weight gain is lipoprotein lipase (LPL), which is produced by fat cells and helps them store fat. LPL responds to sex-linked hormones: estrogen in women and testosterone in men.

In women, the hips, breasts and thighs churn out LPL. The thighs and buttocks are repositories for long-term fat storage. In men, it's their mid-section that makes LPL. But these fat cells are for quick energy, explaining in part why a man can pare down his belly faster than a woman can slim down her hips.

Here are a handful of studies that illustrate the genetic connection to weight gain as research in this field continues:

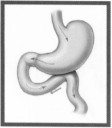

David Klemm
Normal stomach

• One study of 673 pairs of identical and fraternal Swedish twins who had been raised both together and apart set out to discover whether body mass was determined by nature or nuture. Identical twins have the same genetic makeup while fraternal twins are as close as typical siblings. The results were reported in the May 24, 1990, issue of the New England Journal of Medicine: The identical twins' weight varied little whether they were raised together or apart. But fraternal twins, even those who grew up together with the same environmental influences, were far less likely to share similar body weights.

• In that same issue, a small study suggested that some people are more prone to gain weight than others. Twelve pairs of young adult male twins ate an extra 1,000 calories a week for 100 days. Over that time, the twins gained between 9 and 29 pounds. But the weight gain and distribution was identical in each twin pair, suggesting a strong genetic component in how the extra calories were handled by the body.

• In a pioneering study at a Vermont prison conducted by Ethan Sims at the University of Vermont and discussed by Gina Kolata in *Rethinking Thin* (Picador, 2007), volunteers who had never been fat forced themselves to gain weight, eating as much as they could every day with their intake carefully monitored by the researchers. Once these men were 20 to 25 percent over their normal weight, their metabolsim shot up by 50 percent. At the study's end, they had no trouble losing the gained pounds.

Does the LAP-BAND® involve cutting, stapling or bypassing your stomach?

No. Other forms of weight-loss surgery do employ these techniques. The LAP-BAND® involves a small amount of stitching: To help the band stay in place, it is stitched around your stomach. But no permanent changes are made to the body's physiology.

Can the LAP-BAND® be removed?

Yes. Although it's not meant to be removed, it can be. In most cases, this operation can also be done laparoscopically. The stomach generally returns to its original shape once the band is removed. After removal, though, if you revert to your old eating habits, you may gain back the weight you have lost and perhaps more.

The researchers think that the men's metabolism went into overdrive to get their weight back down to the body's comfort zone. We also know that metabolism can slow way down when heavy people lose weight. So the body's metabolism may speed up or slow down to keep weight within a set range.

• In the laboratory, mice can be bred to be very obese. (They look like powder puffs.) This is the result of a defect in a single gene, called the "ob" gene, which is associated with the ability to make a hormone called leptin. The problem in humans is much more complicated genetically, with more than 100 genes involved in some aspect of obesity, but leptin is suspected of playing an important role.

Current research tells us in a variety of ways that overweight and obesity are physiological problems, not motivational ones. We believe that one day research may uncover a better way to lose weight than with LAP-BAND® surgery. But for now, we know of no more effective means for severely overweight and obese people to take off pounds and keep them off – without trade-offs for other health problems.

To understand why we say that, let's look at the other major weight-loss surgery techniques currently available in the U.S., as well as a relatively new technique that's gaining attention.

Gastric bypass

Probably the best-known gastric weight-loss surgery is gastric bypass, which has been covered a lot in the media and in books. This is how TV personalities Al Roker and Star Jones lost so much weight. You may hear it referred to as Roux-en-Y gastric bypass surgery.

With gastric bypass, surgeons create a pouch about the size of an egg from the

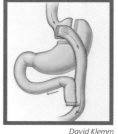

David Klemm
Gastric bypass procedure

What are some of the complications associated with the LAP-BAND® System?

Complications are rare, but they do come up. These include band slippage, band erosion, tubing leakage, port infection and esophageal dilation. In the U.S. Food and Drug Administration clinical trials, complications were more common than they are now, as techniques have improved. To screen for possible complications, patients should undergo an esophogastroduodenoscopy each year. During this 15-minute procedure, the patient is lightly sedated and a scope takes pictures down the throat and swallowing tube to check the location of the band. It's especially important in detecting erosion, an asymptomatic condition where the band begins to work through the wall of the stomach.

top of your stomach. It becomes your new stomach. The surgeon then takes a piece of your intestine and connects this small pouch to the rest of your intestines at a point down past your stomach.

With this surgery, you bypass the largest portion of the stomach entirely. The bypassed portion of the stomach is left in place but will no longer be used to digest food. With bypass surgery, you eat a small amount of food and feel full as the stomach pouch stretches and sends the message to your brain to stop eating. Then the food travels down this connecting piece of intestine, which produces no digestive juices to break the food down.

Before the bypass hooks back up with the intestinal tract, stomach acids, pancreatic juices, and bile continue to be secreted into the intestines.

These ultimately mix with the food where the bypass attaches to the rest of the intestinal tract. Food is digested, but some nutrients, such as B12, iron, calcium and folate, must be supplemented because they are normally absorbed through the stomach. So is a large portion of the protein we eat.

With gastric bypass, you do eat less and you do lose weight. And there are surgeons who are very good at performing this operation, which has a longer history than the LAP-BAND® system. Besides eating less, you also lose weight because you don't absorb all the calories from the food you do eat.

Unfortunately, you also don't absorb many of the vitamins and nutrients your body requires. You also lose weight due to something called dumping syndrome: A bypass patient who eats anything with sugar in it becomes very ill.

Dumping syndrome can cause nausea and vomiting, diarrhea, a bloated feeling, dizziness, and sweating. It is not overstating to say that you feel like you're going to die. This occurs because the particular stretch of intestine that makes up the bypass isn't accustomed to handling sugar. The reaction is so unpleasant that if you eat a candy bar or something else sugary, you won't want to do it again. But as time goes by, the intestines do adapt, to the point where you can eat sugar without this negative reaction.

Under these conditions, you lose weight quickly. Gastric bypass patients can lose 100 pounds in three months. They look like they are shrinking almost before your eyes. So it is an effective weight-loss surgery.

But other aspects of bypass are problematic. Foremost, slightly more than one out of 50 people (2.6 percent) who get the bypass die within five years of the surgery, according to a 2007 study that looked at all bariatric surgery patients in Pennsylvania (Omalu, B. I. et. al. Death Rates and Causes of Death After Bariatric Surgery for Pennsylvania Residents, 1995 to 2004. Arch Surg (2007); 142(10):923-929).

Those are not very favorable odds. Another problem is that certain essential amino acids that are normally absorbed by the stomach must be consumed in another form. Bypass patients also can eventually gain weight back as the pouch stretches and as the dumping effect wears off. Patients sometimes have to undergo revision surgery to re-size the pouch.

And while gastric bypass is reversible, the reversal procedure is very complicated and risky. Few surgeons are willing to tackle it. Reconnecting the stomach is far more difficult than disconnecting it. So the surgery is rarely performed. Once you get your guts rerouted, you're pretty much rerouted for life.

Stomach stapling

Stapling is another form of gastric weight-loss surgery, but it's falling out of favor with most surgeons. In stapling, sometimes called vertical banded gastroplasty, surgical staples and a plastic band are used to create a pouch at the top of the stomach that can hold about 1 cup of food before you feel full. This pouch is

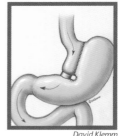

David Klemm
Stomach stapling procedure

not completely closed off from the rest of the stomach.

So, as with the LAP-BAND®, a small opening allows the contents of the pouch to flow into the stomach, where it can be digested and moved along to the small intestine.

With stapling, you do eat less, and you will lose weight initially. But it has been found that the staples sometimes break through, and this makes it possible to eat more and gain back lost weight. Stomach stapling is seldom done anymore.

Sleeve gastrectomy

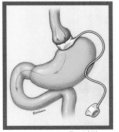

Sleeve gastrectomy

Lapband procedure

The sleeve gastrectomy is a relatively new procedure that's used with certain patients for whom the LAP-BAND® is not appropriate. Patients who can't follow-up properly with diet, who have an aversion to an implant or have immune problems requiring the use of steroids are candidates for the sleeve gastrectomy. So, too, are the rare patients who have erosion or infection problems which can occur with the LAP-BAND®.

The stomach is a kidney-shaped organ. When a sleeve gastrectomy is performed, the surgeon takes away part of the stomach to make it a banana-shaped organ. There's less stomach to fill up, and the stomach that remains functions normally. It still churns, produces acid and absorbs nutrients as it should.

The sleeve gastrectomy is major surgery and does require a hospital stay. The risk is higher than with the LAP-BAND®, less than with bypass, and it is permanent. The weight-loss results are similar to bypass and the band.

Advantages of the LAP-BAND®

Now that we have explained the most common forms of gastric weight-loss surgery, let us expand on why we prefer the LAP-BAND®:

• The LAP-BAND® involves minimally invasive surgery – usually performed at an outpatient surgical center. The band is put in place laparoscopically. You'll go home the same day, and you'll be able to return to work in as few as three days, if necessary.

• Your stomach remains intact: LAP-BAND® surgery involves no cutting or stapling on your stomach.

• The band is adjustable. When it is tightened, it increases satiety and encourages you to gradually eat less. It

What about the long term?

Scientists are just beginning to produce the first longer-term studies with both the adjustable gastric band and gastric bypass. We say adjustable gastric band because some of the foreign studies are using different bands from the LAP-BAND.®

Several studies are available from Australian researchers, including one of the largest, which covers 10 years and more than 100,000 patients (O'Brien, P. and Dixon, J.B. Lap-band: Outcomes and Results. J Laparendosc Adv Surg Tech A 2003 Aug;13(4): 265-70).

As more studies accrue, the adjustable gastric band and gastric bypass are demonstrating nearly equal long-term outcomes for loss, about 65 percent of excess weight after five years. Gastric bypass patients do lose weight faster.

But around the world in countries that offer both weight-loss surgeries, there is a growing preference for the band.

In Europe, Australia and Mexico, the band is now preferred about 75 percent of the time.

can also be loosened to let more food flow through - something you would want if you were pregnant, for example.

• Your digestive tract is not rerouted. Your stomach is not surgically altered.

• Your digestive processes remain intact: The food you eat still passes through the lower stomach and the full length of the intestine.
• Nutrients are fully absorbed, the same

as before banding.

• You do not experience dumping syndrome, the initial negative reaction to sugar that occurs after bypass surgery.

• LAP-BAND® surgery is easily reversible. If, for some reason, you wanted or needed to have the band removed, the procedure for doing so is safe and relatively simple.
• You continue seeing your LAP-BAND®

doctor after surgery. This is one of the most important aspects of banding. Because the band is adjustable, you can use the feedback from your body to customize the band's restriction and control the rate of your weight loss. It's not one-size-fits-all. A continuing relationship with your surgeon is vital because it keeps you on track with your weight-loss goal and ensures that you have the support you need to adapt to your band and lose weight successfully. Unless you have a problem, chances are you will have no contact with your bypass or stapling surgeon after the operation.

If you're thinking you'd like to know more, the next step is determining whether you qualify for the surgery. You have to be both heavy enough and healthy enough, and you have to be highly motivated. Dallas bus driver Sylvia Thompson, whose story leads off the next chapter, had the determination. The question was: Would her doctors give her the OK?

Sylvia: Determination trumps ills

Before my LAP-BAND® procedure

After my LAP-BAND® procedure

Chapter 3 | Who's a Candidate for the LAP-BAND®, and What Happens Next

For most of her adult life, bus driver Sylvia Thompson had been an acceptable weight. But a series of medical problems starting in the early '90s changed that. "I had back surgery in 1995. Four discs were fused. They took bone from my hip area to support my spine. I had to use a walker and a back brace. I couldn't do anything for myself. It was a bad time for me. I was in a bad marriage, too."

Before the surgery, doctors gave her steroids and anti-inflammatory drugs as well as antidepressants. "They were trying to do everything they could to relieve the pain without doing the surgery," Sylvia says. To no avail. She would have the surgery, and she would continue taking pain medication for years.

Before her serious medical problems, Sylvia's weight had crept up to 150, but she still was able to carry this comfortably on her 5-foot-10-inch frame. But her continuing back problems led her to put on weight, and her weight compounded her physical ills. She developed a thyroid problem that required surgical removal in 2000. By then, Sylvia's weight had ballooned to 254 pounds.

Still, Sylvia was determined to rebuild her life. "I had had my pity party," she says. "I just got tired of being sick and tired and being at home.

I was doing a little bit of everything to get me back where I wanted to be."

One of those things was making up her mind that she was going to drive a bus again. She had become a dispatcher when her back gave out. Slowly, on her own, she also started weaning herself off the many medications she was taking. And she ditched the bad marriage.

Sylvia met her second husband at the transit company, and they were married in 2002. But still she struggled with her weight.

One day while waiting at the end of the line on her bus route, she read a magazine story about Dr. Jayaseelan and the LAP-BAND®. "When I saw the picture of how large the woman was, and read how she had had the surgery and lost all that weight, I wanted to cry."

She decided to get the LAP-BAND®, but she had

How do I know if I'm a candidate for the LAP-BAND®?

To be eligible for surgery, you must be at least 50 pounds overweight. Insurance requires a Body Mass Index of 40 or higher. People with risk (or co-morbidity) factors such as joint pain, gastroesophageal reflux disease (GERD), hypertension, or high cholesterol, may qualify with a BMI of 35 or higher. Surgeons will accept some self-pay patients with a BMI as low as 30. You should be in reasonably good health, and you should provide your doctor with a complete medical history, including current and past medical problems. Although there is no age restriction, banding patients under 18 is generally evaluated on a case-by-case basis and may be performed only with the approval of a parent or guardian.

one physical hurdle that determination couldn't overcome. Her doctors had concerns about her heart. They thought she had a blockage and, if that were true, she would not be allowed to have the surgery. Fortunately, further evaluation showed her heart was fine, and Sylvia got her band in October 2005. She has never looked back.

The only medication she takes today is for her thyroid. And she has lost 89 pounds since getting banded. At her largest, she was a size 18. Now she's a 6. "About six months ago," she says, "I needed an outfit for a funeral. I ran up to Marshalls and picked out five suits, in sizes 8 and 10. I began trying them on, and the sales clerk said, 'Why, that suit is cute on you, but it's way too big.' She went out and got a size 6. I couldn't believe I wore a size 6." That's where Sylvia remains today, and she's happily married and driving her bus.

Most people considering the LAP-BAND® have been told by their doctors that they need to lose weight or risk early death. That's strong motivation, but what Sylvia's story illustrates is a stronger motivation still.

We encounter it often and call it the Fed-Up Factor: People are fed up with their weight and the burdens it imposes, fed up with the social limitations, fed up with hurting and feeling bad, and fed up with their own perceived failure to lose weight by conventional means. They are so fed up that they are willing to undergo weight-loss surgery, and they see it as their last, best hope.

The band requires the motivation to change. It is a powerful tool, but it won't work without your participation and effort. Most surgeons will not agree to perform the LAP-BAND® procedure unless you are willing to make the necessary lifestyle and dietary changes that go along with it.

Sylvia was determined to succeed. She understood the 70-30 split: The band would do 70 percent of the work and effectively restrict the amount of food she ate. But she had to do the other 30 percent.

The band limits how much you can eat at a time, but it can't stop you from driving to a fast-food outlet for a shake. That is your job. The band can't stop you from drinking high-calorie beverages or sipping high-fat soups that slide easily past the band.

The band will help you feel full on less food. But you have to follow the guidelines for what to eat and how to eat.

That brings up another key point: Once you're banded, your relationship to food changes. Food begins to play a different role in your life. It's important to know that this is part of the process because the change can be surprisingly challenging. In fact, we take up several chapters later discussing what this means.

Once your surgeon is convinced that you've got the right frame of mind,

How do I know the LAP-BAND® will work for me?
*It's important to understand that the LAP-BAND® works **with** you, not **for** you. Once you're banded, you must be willing and able to follow your doctor's advice about what to eat and how to eat. An exercise program is highly recommended. So is participation in an after-care program, where possible. It is also necessary to follow-up with office visits according to the schedule you and your doctor set.*

What are the up-front costs?
Prior to surgery, the only up-front expense will be for the cost of your pre-operative testing. In the United States, these tests can run $500 or more, depending on how and where they are done. The cost is usually covered by health insurance.

The more overweight you are, the more you are at risk for the following problems, according to the Centers for Disease Control and Prevention. People with a BMI of 35 to 39, defined as severely obese, may qualify for gastric-banding surgery if some of these risk factors are present.

• **High blood pressure** – Defined as a systolic reading of 140 (pressure generated when your heart beats) over a diastolic reading of 90 (pressure in your blood vessels when the heart is at rest). Increases your risk for heart attack and stroke. Losing a significant amount of weight, as LAP-BAND® patients typically do, often improves blood pressure to the point where you can reduce or eliminate medication, with your doctor's consent.

• **High cholesterol & triglycerides** – Indicate the presence of too many fatty substances in your blood and increase your risk for heart attack and coronary artery disease, also called hardening of the arteries. LAP-BAND® patients who lose a lot of weight significantly improve their lipid profile.

• **Osteoarthritis** – People with this degenerative disease of the joints usually have joint pain and some limitation of movement. LAP-BAND® patients who lose weight report less pain and improved range of motion.

• **Type 2 diabetes** – Marked by high blood sugar levels. Over time, can damage nerves and blood vessels, and lead to heart disease, stroke, blindness, kidney disease, nerve problems and, in extreme cases, renal failure and limb amputation. The LAP-BAND® can eliminate diabetes or reduce the amount of medication necessary to control it. Long-time, insulin-dependent type 2 diabetics will see a reduction in necessary medications, but may not eliminate them entirely.

• **Coronary heart disease and heart attack** – CHD is damage to blood vessels, often narrowed by plaque buildup associated with too much low-density lipoprotein (LDL). When the buildup causes a blockage in one or more of the vessels of the heart, a heart attack results. Part of the heart muscle dies in a heart attack. The

LAP-BAND® can't undo damage that's already done, but losing weight with the band, following a heart-healthy diet and exercising can prevent further damage.

- **Stroke** – A blood vessel carrying blood to the brain develops a clot, blocking flow (ischemic stroke), or a blood vessel bursts, leaking blood into the brain (hemorrhagic stroke). The resulting lower blood pressure that comes from losing weight with the LAP-BAND® can reduce your risk of a stroke.

- **Sleep apnea and respiratory problems** – With sleep apnea, you stop breathing for at least 10 seconds at a time while you're asleep. Episodes can occur hundreds of times a night. Other respiratory problems include shortness of breath and asthma. All of these conditions show improvement with the kind of weight loss reported using the LAP-BAND®.

- **Some cancers** – Obesity has been linked to breast, endometrial, ovarian, colon, and prostate cancers. Losing significant weight is one factor that

can reduce the risk of these cancers. In addition, we regularly encounter patients with these problems, which are not life-threatening, but nevertheless important to quality of life:

- **Female fertility problems** – Excess weight and obesity can interfere with female hormones and make it harder to get pregnant. Losing weight helps restore your hormone balance and make it easier to conceive.

- **Acid-reflux disease** – Excessive stomach fat can push on your stomach and cause acid to come back up in your esophagus. The placement of the LAP-BAND® can relieve acid reflux immediately.

- **Frequent urination** – Too much weight on your bladder can cause you to want to urinate more often. Losing weight relieves the pressure on your bladder.

What's involved with pre-operative testing, and where can I have it done?

Pre-op exams are required before any surgery can be scheduled. These tests may include an upper gastrointestinal series, an electrocardiogram, a chest X-ray, and blood and urine analysis. These tests can be done by a laboratory or hospital. Most patients simply go through their primary-care physician.

Can I have the LAP-BAND® procedure done if I've already had gallbladder surgery?

Yes, providing the pre-op tests reveal no other problems.

qualifying for the band comes down to your health and weight. Specifically, if you are at least 50 pounds overweight or have a Body Mass Index of 40 or higher (defined as morbidly obese) and are in reasonably good health, you will qualify for the LAP-BAND® procedure.

Some people may qualify with a BMI of 35 to 39 (defined as severely obese) if other life-threatening risk factors are present. They still have to be reasonably healthy, but may also be dealing with the following: high blood pressure, osteoarthritis, high cholesterol and triglycerides, type 2 diabetes, coronary heart disease, gallbladder disease, sleep apnea, respiratory problems, or some cancers.

In some cases, a patient with a BMI between 30 and 34 (defined as obese) can

make a case for having the surgery.

Why is Body Mass Index so important? It's a scientific measure we use to tell us how much overweight (or underweight) people are. If you're uncertain of your BMI, go to the chart on Page 30 and locate your height and weight.

Someone with a BMI between 19 and 24.9 is considered to be of normal weight. Overweight is defined as 25 to 29. BMI is determined the same way for men and women. The only group BMI doesn't accurately describe is super-athletes, who can have a high BMI while their body-fat percentage remains low.

If your weight qualifies you for the LAP-BAND® and you're in relatively good health, you'll undergo several pre-op tests before your surgery is scheduled. These can include an upper gastrointestinal series, an electrocardiogram, a chest X-ray, and blood and urine analysis. Only after your surgeon is satisfied with the results on these tests will your operation be scheduled.

The pre-operation diet

Prior to your surgery, you'll be asked to follow a no-fat, low-sugar diet. Not every doctor will require the same diet or duration; it varies from practice to practice. It's our experience that following the diet for seven days produces the best results.

The purpose of eating this way is to shrink your liver so that the surgeon can gain easy access to your stomach. The liver, which is the largest organ inside you, is a big triangle that sits on your stomach. It processes cholesterol, among other functions. Without the pre-op diet, it's so big that it completely covers the stomach, making surgery much more difficult. But after the special diet, the liver shrinks to

Do I have to follow any special diet before the surgery?

Yes. The exact diet and length of time vary from doctor to doctor. In our approach, we ask patients to eat a low-fat, low-sugar, high-protein liquid diet seven days prior to surgery. The reason: This shrinks the liver and makes it much easier and safer for the surgeon to put the LAP-BAND® in place.

It's not an easy diet to follow. But the doctor will know right away if you have cheated when he looks inside with a scope. Even though you may be prepped and ready to go, he may postpone the surgery until you can commit to the diet. Generally, the diet allows liquids such as water, sports drinks, tea, coffee, frozen nonfat dessert bars such as Popsicles, broth (vegetable, chicken or beef), Jell-O, Crystal Light, skim milk, clear juices, such as apple juice, and low-carb protein shakes.

If I need gallbladder surgery, can I have the LAP-BAND® put in place during the same operation?

No. It's best to have these procedures done separately, as the gallbladder surgery may infect your LAP-BAND® if the surgeries are done concurrently.

Body Mass Index Chart

Weight in Pounds

Height in Feet and Inches	120	130	140	150	160	170	180	190	200	210	220	230	240	250
4'6	29	31	34	36	39	41	43	46	48	51	53	56	58	60
4'8	27	29	31	34	36	38	40	43	45	47	49	52	54	56
4'10	25	27	29	31	34	36	38	40	42	44	46	48	50	52
5'0	23	25	27	29	31	33	35	37	39	41	43	45	47	49
5'2	22	24	26	27	29	31	33	35	37	38	40	42	44	46
5'4	21	22	24	26	28	29	31	33	34	36	38	40	41	43
5'6	19	21	23	24	26	27	29	31	32	34	36	37	39	40
5'8	18	20	21	23	24	26	27	29	30	32	34	35	37	38
5'10	17	19	20	22	23	24	26	27	29	30	32	33	35	36
6'0	16	18	19	20	22	23	24	26	27	28	30	31	33	34
6'2	15	17	18	19	21	22	23	24	26	27	28	30	31	32
6'4	15	16	17	18	20	21	22	23	24	26	27	28	29	30
6'6	14	15	16	17	19	20	21	22	23	24	25	27	28	29
6'8	13	14	15	17	18	19	20	21	22	23	24	25	26	28

Healthy Weight   Overweight   Obese

Note: This chart is for adults (aged 20 years and older).
Source: U.S. Surgeon General.

where it looks like a baby's liver. Then the surgeon can easily move it out of the way and slip the LAP-BAND® in place.

The pre-op diet isn't easy. This is another reason why commitment is so important.

In our approach, you're limited to clear liquids and low-carbohydrate protein drinks. These include water, tea, coffee, sugar-free frozen dessert pops such as Popsicles, broth (vegetable, chicken and beef), won-ton soup (without the won-ton), sugar-free Jell-O, low-carbohydrate protein shakes (limit: two a day), Crystal Light, nonfat milk, clear juices and lactose-free protein drinks, such as Isopure.

We ask you to follow this diet for seven days because that's how long it takes for your liver to start tapping its fat stores, which is what prompts it to shrink.

This is not a diet you can cheat on.

Your surgeon will know as soon as he looks inside with a scope whether you followed the diet. If you haven't, he will likely postpone your surgery until after you can commit to the diet.

The evening before your surgery, your anesthesiologist will contact you to go over your medications and let you know which ones to take the day of surgery. You'll also be asked not to eat or drink anything after midnight. Then, all you'll need to do is get a good night's sleep before the big day.

But for some people, that night before is not an easy one. Some people are scared of any surgery. That was the case for Mary Belle Turner, whose story leads off the next chapter.

Mary Belle: Overcoming her fear of surgery

Before my LAP-BAND® procedure

After my LAP-BAND® procedure

Chapter 4 | Preparing for the Day of Surgery

"I'd never had surgery," says Mary Belle Turner, a 27-year-old program director for surgical weight-loss patients. "I didn't know what to expect. My concern was mainly the surgery part and general anesthesia." The closer she got to the day of surgery, the more anxiety the Dallas woman felt. And although her parents were supportive, her father let her know that she could change her mind, right up to the last minute. But by the day in 2005 when her operation was scheduled, Mary Belle was determined to go through with it. "I was afraid," she says, "but committed."

"I've been heavy my entire life," she says. "I was diagnosed with high blood pressure at 16 and was on two meds for that." High blood pressure runs in her family, she says, "but the weight certainly added to it." Mary Belle is 5-feet-9-inches tall and weighed 332 pounds at her heaviest.

"I was rapidly approaching the largest size at the plus-size stores, and I didn't know where I was going to shop next." She also knew she wasn't going to hide herself inside big, baggy clothes; she was too young for that.

"I reached a point," she says, "where I just knew that I wanted to lose the weight. People finally get to a point where they're not happy with themselves." She looked into bypass surgery, *"but I just couldn't get comfortable with it,"* she says. Then she saw an ad for the LAP-BAND® and signed up to attend an informational seminar.

"I called and talked my mom into coming with me. I had to have my parents' support and approval to do this. I wouldn't have felt comfortable doing it without them."

The seminar, where Dr. Jayaseelan spoke, helped Mary Belle confirm that she wanted to go through with the procedure, and her mother, while still apprehensive, began to warm to the idea. Her father, though, took more convincing. *"Eventually, everyone came around and realized it would be a good thing."*

How long does the surgery take?

LAP-BAND® surgery is usually performed at an outpatient clinic. It takes about 30 minutes to an hour.

What are the risk factors during and immediately following the LAP-BAND® surgery?

Any gastric operation for obesity is major surgery and carries with it the same risks inherent in any operation. The same is true of the LAP-BAND® procedure.

• In a small number of cases, infection can develop around the band or at the site where the port is placed under the skin; your doctor will be able to determine fairly quickly if this happens.

• The port or the band might leak and need to be replaced, although this is rare.

• The risk of dying during the operation is small (1 in 2,500), but there is a slight risk of either a heart attack or a life-threatening blood clot that passes into the lungs (pulmonary embolism).

Mary Belle's parents came to stay with her the night before and went with her early the next morning to the surgery center. They were at her side as soon as she woke up.

"When I came out of surgery, I was really groggy and nauseous. Really out of it. They were all saying, 'You've got to get up and walk,' and I said, 'You've got to be kidding me.'"

Still, she was home by noon. "I slept a little bit, but then my mom had me up walking and taking the pain medication and Gas-X, trying to make me as comfortable as possible."

In a little over a year, Mary Belle lost 150 pounds and has kept the weight off. It has changed her life.

"I'm more outgoing and confident," she says. "I feel more myself than when I was heavy." Six months after she was banded, her doctor also took her off her blood-pressure medications.

Today, she shops at regular clothing stores. She gets to tell her story often, as she works with patients at a company that *specializes in the LAP-BAND® procedure. And even though she's been successful at maintaining her weight, she's still adjusting to her new size and look.*

She knew, once she made up her mind to do it, that she couldn't back out of the surgery, no matter how scary going under the anesthesia had seemed. "I would be sick if I hadn't done it," she says. "I knew I would feel that way. It's just taking that leap."

✉

The day of surgery is one of the most exciting in your LAP-BAND® journey. With surgery, you take the big step: One moment you are without the band. The next moment you have it.

Not every practice will be the same, but here's what the day of surgery is like with Dr. Jayaseelan.

After successfully completing your pre-op diet, you will arrive at the surgery center an hour before your procedure to complete paperwork. We encourage you to bring lip balm and a small pillow for use after your surgery.

In the pre-op area, the nurse will discuss the operation with you again and start an intravenous line. Ninety-nine percent of the time, this is pain-free. The doctor will then talk to you and

Will having the LAP-BAND® affect the other medications that I take?

You will be able to continue taking prescription medication, but you may need to switch to capsules, or break big tablets in half or dissolve them in water so they don't get stuck and make you sick. Always ask the doctor who prescribes your medicine about this.

Your surgeon also may tell you to avoid taking aspirin and other nonsteroidal, anti-inflammatory drugs that relieve pain. These include ibuprofen (Advil and Motrin), naproxen sodium (Aleve), and ketoprofen (Orudis KT). NSAIDs can cause erosion if they sit in the upper pouch and break down. This wears away the lining of your stomach.

If you need to take something for pain, acetaminophen (Tylenol and Panadol) is a good choice. And if for some reason you must take NSAIDs, your doctor will prescribe something such as Protonix (pantoprazole sodium) to offset the effects of the NSAIDs.

Are there any short-term side effects of the operation?

Adjustable gastric banding is tolerated well by most patients. Complication rates are low, but short-term side effects do occasionally occur. The following are the most common:

• ***Spitting up.*** *Most patients will occasionally feel pain or will spit up after swallowing food. In most cases, this is caused by trying to eat too much too quickly. After banding, you will learn to chew your food more slowly and thoroughly and to listen to your body's signals. You should refrain from eating for two hours if you feel nauseated, have pain, or spit up; this gives your stomach, which likely has swollen, time to heal. Vomiting, which is a more violent response than spitting up, is a warning sign that something is not right and should be discussed with your surgeon. It can be caused by not eating correctly or because the opening between the pouch and the main part of the stomach has become too narrow. This means the band may need to be adjusted.*

• ***Constipation.*** *Some patients feel constipated after surgery. This is mainly caused by the reduced food intake, which results in less waste matter, and thus fewer bowel movements. It is normal to experience a reduction in volume in your stools, as well. If you do find it necessary to take a laxative, avoid the so-called bulking type. Use liquid laxatives instead, such as milk of magnesia. Also, be sure you're drinking plenty of water or the equivalent. Needs vary, but we recommend a minimum of eight (8-ounce) glasses a day. If you continue to feel constipated, check with your doctor.*

• ***Hair loss.*** *Some patients experience hair loss during the first six months after surgery. This is caused by the reduction in caloric intake, which your body interprets as starvation. This, however, never leads to baldness, and normal hair growth will eventually return. Most often, hair loss is associated with insufficient protein in the diet. We recommend that patients consume at least 60 grams of protein daily.*

How long will it take to recover?

Because LAP-BAND® surgery is usually a laparoscopic procedure, patients typically spend less than 24 hours at an outpatient surgical center. Most patients need a week of home recovery before returning to work, although it is possible in some cases to schedule the surgery on Friday and return to work the following Monday. Surgeons' instructions vary, but generally you will be asked not to lift anything heavier than 20 pounds for six weeks.

Is there any scarring from the surgery?

Because laparoscopic surgery is minimally invasive, there is very little scarring. In most cases, you will have several small incisions that will heal very quickly.

your family prior to the procedure to make sure all your questions have been answered. Then the anesthesiologist will come and talk with you. Because this is an exciting time, the doctor will give you something to relax.

The next thing you know, you're in the recovery room, asking, "When am I going to surgery?" Now you will be ready for the lip balm, as your lips will be very dry. Many patients at this point don't believe they've had the surgery yet, but we assure them they have. Modern surgery is all about making the process as pleasant as possible for the patient, so it's easier to go through than it used to be.

We use tiny incisions so you'll be able to get up and around immediately after the procedure. Some of our patients have surgery on Friday and go back to work on Monday, although recovery is probably easier if you give yourself a little more time off to heal.

After you wake up, it may take a moment for the fact to sink in: You're banded now.

You will have some pain after the surgery. Some patients describe the pain as akin to how you'd feel after doing a hundred sit-ups. This is where the pillow comes in: It feels good to hold it against your side, where you've had the incisions, during the ride home.

Some patients also experience shoulder pain, or pain in other parts of their bodies, which is caused by gas. To deal with any post-operative pain, you will be given a

Is it true that I might have shoulder pain after surgery? Why is this?

Gas can get trapped in your body. Some people experience gas pain, and others don't. There's no clear reason why some people get this. To help move the gas out of your body and relieve the pain, start moving around as much as possible as soon after surgery as you reasonably can. Get up and walk; do a lap around the house every hour that you are awake. Gas-relief products such as Gas-X can help, too. The gas pain should go away completely in a few weeks.

Why do I feel sore longer around the port area after surgery?

The port site incision is the largest cut, and the port is stitched to the abdominal muscle, which takes time to heal. The tubing passes through the muscle into the abdominal cavity, where it connects to the band. This is why reaching down the left side or making certain movements may be difficult for the first four to eight weeks. Once everything is healed, you shouldn't feel any soreness.

prescription for pain medication, as well as anti-nausea medication, when you leave the surgery center.

The initial pain will pass. But you can actively diminish your pain and prevent complications by following these "must do's" after surgery.

Must-do's after surgery
• **Walking.** It is very important that you **walk for five minutes every hour** you're awake to keep the blood circulating in your legs. This is something you must do, even if you don't feel like it.

We understand that moving around right after surgery feels uncomfortable and that you will want to go home and go straight to bed. But that can be very dangerous: When you lie still for a long time, the blood stagnates in your legs and can turn into a clot. This blood clot can travel up to your lungs and kill you.

It is helpful if you have a friend or

family member who can stay with you and be your cheerleader and motivator through the first 24 hours and get you up and moving around.

When it's bedtime, you can then go to bed for a normal eight hours. The next day, get up and pretend that you didn't have surgery. The more you get up and around, the more quickly your pain will diminish and you'll be able to return to your usual activities.

Here are the only things you can't do: For the first four to six weeks, don't lift anything heavier than 20 pounds as this may lead to a hernia. The other no-no: For two weeks after surgery, no tub baths, hot tubs or swimming because the water may seep into your wounds. But you can

How soon after surgery can I start exercising?

You should begin walking right after surgery. After four weeks, the usual healing period, you should be able to resume, or begin, a regular exercise program.

I hear people use the terms vomiting, spitting up and sliming. What do these mean?

• *Vomiting is just what it sounds like: The contents of the stomach, mixed with stomach acid, come back up the esophagus in spasms.*

• *Spitting up occurs when the contents of the pouch, for whatever reason, can't pass through the opening to the stomach. This could happen because of insufficient chewing, for example. Because the contents of the pouch haven't passed into the stomach, they haven't yet mixed with gastric juices. So they come back up like a baby's spit-up.*

• *Sliming is when you eat more than your pouch can easily hold or the food isn't completely chewed, your body senses that there is something it needs to deal with. The stomach will first try to work it through by producing mucous and extra saliva to help it slip on down, hence the term sliming. Failing that, the food will come back up. Sliming is your body's way of forcefully saying "STOP" or "Sit back and stop eating now." Sometimes you slime so much that you spit up. If that happens, you will have plenty of time to excuse yourself and leave the table. At other times, you will stop before this happens.*

and should start showering the day after surgery.

• **Deep breathing. Take ten deep breaths every hour**. This is also very important for healing.

After surgery, it will hurt to take a deep breath, and patients often breathe shallowly as a result. Some whisper or even ring a bell for assistance rather than take a deep breath and call out. This, too, can be dangerous because with shallow breathing, part of your lungs is not expanding and getting air. This can lead to fever and lung complications.

So make it part of your recovery program to do the required deep breathing every hour. A pillow placed across your abdomen will give it some support and help you with deep breathing and coughing.

Other post-op suggestions

• Make sure you have some milk of magnesia and Gas-X on hand. After surgery, gas can build up in your bowels and other parts of your body. As we mentioned, it is not unusual to experience some shoulder pain after surgery, which is gas. This is all normal, and over-the-counter drugs can help.

• Follow the post-op diet detailed in the next chapter to minimize the natural churning of your stomach so that everything heals properly.

• To prevent infection, keep your incisions clean with soap and water. If you like, apply some Neosporin, but only after the incisions have healed over.

Sometimes, to lighten things up, we also tell our patients, "No mud wrestling for a month." We say it in jest, but the truth is, getting banded can be so exhilarating at first that patients want to rush out and do everything at once.

We call this the honeymoon with the band because it has that same euphoric quality. And when you hear the stories of people like Betty Eads, whose story leads off the next chapter, their enthusiasm is contagious.

Betty: It's never too late

Before my LAP-BAND® procedure

After my LAP-BAND® procedure

Chapter 5 | The Honeymoon: Learning How to Eat

For Betty Eads, the LAP-BAND® honeymoon has never ended despite having to work with a slip. "I'm still very excited," she says, after five years. This stands in contrast to the woman who, by her own description, was so withdrawn before getting banded that her world consisted of going to work and returning to her Lewisville, Texas, home. At her heaviest, Betty weighed 274 pounds on a 5-foot-2-inch frame. On her long-ago wedding day, she had weighed just 102 pounds. In between, there were babies. "After my first son was born, I never really lost that weight," she says. "I stayed at 150." She and her husband ended up with three sons. Although overweight, Betty was rocking along well enough until her husband died, leaving her alone. Then began a long, slow tailspin. "I threw myself into work," she says, "and at night I sat on the sofa and ate." Over the course of 20 years, she became highly reclusive. "It got out of hand," Betty says, looking back. "It got to the point where I didn't care if I went anywhere or not."

But on some level Betty knew she had to do something. She was 69, and time was running out. She had tried diets. But every time she lost some weight, it would creep right back. When she did find the will to venture out, she would quickly get winded. She could not even play with her grandchildren; she could only watch.

Then she saw an ad in the newspaper for the LAP-BAND®. One of her sons was in the medical field, and he helped her research the procedure

and ultimately urged her to go for it.

Just getting ready on the pre-op diet, Betty lost about 25 pounds. And right after banding, she could tell an immediate, though not dramatic, difference. Another of her sons took her to Hawaii then for her 70th birthday, and Betty noticed she was able to do a little more and keep up a little better.

Fast-forward through a year of banding. "On my 71st birthday," she says, "I went to Canada with my brother and was able to climb a mountain and do anything he and his wife were able to do." But Betty wasn't done yet. She just kept opening up to new experiences. "The next birthday, at 72," she says, "I went parasailing!"

Then she hit a bump. Betty's band slipped late last year when she had a stomach virus.   For several months after that, she also was dealing with a different illness that meant leaving her repositioned band unfilled. "I gained a good bit of weight back," she says, having put on about 50 pounds. But now she's back on fills and back with the program. "I'm going to do it again. That's for sure."

Thanks to the LAP-BAND®, Betty says, she got her life and her health back. "I have just done so many things, and I'm having a ball. I finally realized that there's more to life than sitting in front of a TV and eating ice cream. ... And I

Do I have to follow a special diet after surgery?

For about a month after surgery, yes. While your stomach heals and adapts to the newly placed band, you'll need to follow a special eating plan. The diet and length of time vary from surgeon to surgeon, but generally require you to be on liquids immediately post-op, followed by the gradual introduction of soft foods, and then solids.

We recommend a liquid diet for two weeks (days 1 to 14). In addition to the liquids you drank on the pre-op diet, you'll be able to add milkshakes, protein shakes, smoothies, V8 and tomato juice, tomato soup, and cream soups. You may wish to avoid acidic juices, such as orange, tomato and grapefruit, during the first two weeks.

The next two weeks (days 15 to 28), you'll add soft foods such as Cream of Wheat, oatmeal, grits, scrambled eggs, mashed potatoes and gravy, yogurt, pudding, applesauce, small-curd cottage cheese, refried beans, and queso (no chips). After the first month, you'll be able to eat pretty much what you like, with the exception of white bread and large chunks of meat, especially well-done beef. You can start eating whatever you wish after the first month. You'll also notice that you quickly get full, which may lead you to evaluate what you eat more carefully.

What if I still feel hungry right after surgery?

Once the swelling goes down during the healing process and before your first fill, it is possible that you will feel very hungry. This varies from person to person, and it's important not to push your stomach too fast into digesting solid foods. We recommend going slow so your stomach won't have to work very hard churning food during the healing phase. Liquids require minimal churning. The same is true for mushy or soft foods. Meat, on the other hand, requires a lot of churning.

If you force the stomach to churn during this healing time, your band may not set securely and you may increase the risk of slippage. Eating less during this period also helps you get a jump on your weight loss, and it can remind you of the commitment you have made to better health.

don't ever want to look like I did before or feel like I did before – ever."

If you are reading this after getting your own LAP-BAND®, congratulations. You have taken the first big step toward losing weight permanently and reclaiming your health. This is when your relationship with the band starts in earnest: We call this the honeymoon because when you come out of surgery, it feels like a fresh, new beginning, with all the promise and hope that a honeymoon holds.

But like a honeymoon, it's really a grace period, wherein you discover a lot about your band and, in the process, yourself.

First, it is an exciting and challenging time filled with new experiences. You may find yourself ravenously hungry at some point. You may be impatient to lose weight faster. You may think you need to eat the way you did before becoming banded and unconsciously size up a meal to fit that need.

But as you begin to transition from the post-op liquid diet to the way you'll eat for the rest of your life, your entire relationship to food will change. Besides learning a new way to eat, you may be surprised to discover just how much time and energy you spent on food before becoming banded.

You may feel alternately angry, ashamed and outraged by this. Your divorce from food starts during this post-op period, and it can be as demanding as a real divorce. But we'll save that for the next chapter. Right

If I feel really hungry during the post-operative healing period, is it OK to cheat just a little and eat some solid foods?

No, it is not. You must be very careful to focus on healing during this post-operative period. Some people get very hungry during this time. Solid foods, especially what we call hard protein, make your stomach churn vigorously. During the healing process, your surgeon wants it to churn as little as possible. It can be helpful to look at the big picture: This is a relatively short period in your life, and your feelings of hunger will diminish. (See "Tick, tick, tick" on Page 68.) Also, most people can do just about anything for a short period of time – just as you were able to stick with the pre-operative diet. Allow yourself more liquids, and find ways other than eating to pass the time.

now, we're all about the honeymoon.

The post-operative diet and healing

In our experience, the healing period following surgery lasts about four weeks. And while the surgery is minimally invasive, it is still surgery and upsets the balance of your body like any wound. The tissue around the band and at the site where the port is attached will be swollen for a time. But as your body heals, it will become accustomed to presence of the band and port, and eventually you'll forget they're there.

When you eat and digest food, you may recall from the first chapter, your stomach churns the food and mixes it with gastric juices so that the nutrients can be extracted.

Protein such as chicken, beef, pork and fish - what we call hard protein - causes the stomach to churn the most vigorously. In contrast, liquids cause the least amount of agitation and churn. Your surgeon will put you on a liquid diet post-surgery to minimize churning, which helps the stomach heal while the LAP-BAND® settles into place. We recommend this all-liquid, post-op diet for 14 days.

During that time, we ask patients to continue on the liquids that were part of the pre-op diet. But now they may add milkshakes, protein shakes, smoothies, V8 and tomato juice, tomato soup, and cream soups. (Some patients avoid acidic juices, such as orange, grapefruit and tomato, during the first two weeks, as these make them feel nauseated.)

Sometimes during this period, as the swelling goes down around the band, you may get so hungry that you think you have to cheat and eat some solid foods.

This does not happen to everyone, but if it happens to you, it's important to find a way to stick with the all-liquid regimen. If you get ravenously hungry, check to be sure you're getting 60 grams of protein each day.

Once I'm over the recovery period, do I have to follow any special diet?

Short answer: No. But because the pouch that's created at the top of your stomach is so much smaller than the stomach you've been used to, you will eat less and you will have to eat differently.

There are some foods you probably will want to avoid. Because white bread, white rice and some pastas soak up saliva and expand in your stomach, they aren't as LAP-BAND® friendly as other foods. The same is true of dried fruits, which can expand and get lodged in the small opening of the stomach pouch. Fibrous foods also have to be approached a little differently. You may wish to go slow with asparagus, pineapple, rhubarb, corn, popcorn, broccoli, some fresh greens and grapes.

*You will also learn not to drink liquids while you eat because two things can happen: First, you can wash the food through your band, which leads you to get hungry sooner. Second, you can "corkscrew" the food in your pouch by placing liquid on top. **In effect, the liquid pushes the solid food down into the opening like a plug, preventing anything from passing through the banded part of the stomach.** And what doesn't go through the band must come back up.*

In general, LAP-BAND® patients improve their digestion if they learn to chew their food well. Most liquids are fine, with the exception of carbonated beverages, as they can cause distension of the stomach pouch which is painful. We recommend that you eat a wide variety of foods – just less volume than before surgery.

You may need to adjust your protein intake with the kind or amount of shake you consume. If you try to slip some solid food in at this stage, you will stimulate the stomach to churn, which may interfere with the band's setting itself around the stomach.

Solid food may also make you throw up, which further jostles the stomach, interferes with healing and can cause slippage. If you experience slippage, the surgeon may need to go in and reset the band. During the post-op recovery period, some people think that because their stomach growls, they must be hungry.

But your stomach will also growl because it is shrinking. If you are getting 60 grams of protein a day spread over three meals, you should be able to live with the level of hunger you experience during this transition.

It is also possible during the first seven days post-op that you will experience some diarrhea or loose stools. This happens because you're essentially putting liquid in, so liquid is more or less what you get out. It is important to stay hydrated during this time.

Alternatively, you may feel constipated. If this is the case, a liquid laxative such as milk of magnesia will usually restore your bowel movements. But don't be surprised if they are overall smaller or less frequent than before you were banded.

Why do some people have difficulty eating 'hard' protein like chicken, fish, ground beef and turkey, even a year after being banded?

Chances are, they are eating too fast. Or, they are not chewing well enough. Whatever isn't small enough to move past the band comes back up. Here's a technique we suggest: Take a small bite of food. Chew the daylights out of it until it's in liquid form. You may feel the need to swallow a couple of times while holding the food in your mouth. Place your tongue on the roof of your mouth and exhale through your nose. Then tip your head back, and allow the chewed-up food to slide down your throat. If, after working with this technique, you still cannot get hard protein down, your band is probably too tight. Also, you might want to put a nickel by your plate to gauge the size of your bites.

What if I feel sick to my stomach after getting banded?

The LAP-BAND® System limits food intake. If you feel nauseated or sick on a regular basis, it may mean that you are not chewing your food well enough or that you are not following the dietary guidelines. Vomiting should be avoided because it can cause slippage. This is where part of the stomach comes up through the band. In rare cases, this requires an operation to reposition the band.

You have drastically reduced the amount of bulk in your system. So smaller, less frequent bowel movements are to be expected.

Moving up to mushies

During the second two weeks post-op, days 15-28, we ask patients to start adding mushies, or soft foods, such as Cream of Wheat, oatmeal, grits, scrambled eggs, mashed potatoes and gravy, yogurt, pudding, applesauce, small-curd cottage cheese, refried beans, and even small amounts of queso (without the chips), if you like.

This is a time when some people start feeling impatient. They want to hurry it up. They want to get the pounds off now. We have seen patients at this juncture express disappointment at losing *only* 15 or 20 pounds. But there's absolutely nothing to be disappointed about, even if you lose no weight.

Healing is the No. 1 priority during this period.

LAP-BAND® eating 101

There's a lot going on when you first start eating solid foods after the four-week healing period. This is when you really learn how to eat with the LAP-BAND® in place.

No more wolfing down a cheeseburger and fries with a cola chaser – not because those are forbidden foods, but because your stomach will hold less food at a time. And you will have to cut your food into smaller bites, as well as chew more thoroughly than you probably ever have before.

In your new banded life, you will need to plan on three small, more or less evenly spaced meals a day. You'll be eating about a cup of food at each meal. We also find that because protein is so important to your energy level and sense of well being, it's best to eat your protein first, followed by your vegetables and finally your starchy

Will I have post-operative problems with eating or bowel movements?

After surgery, you have to learn new eating habits. As you do, you can expect some episodes of spitting up or "PB-ing," otherwise known as "productive burping." The liquid-to-soft-food transition diet should help you adjust to your new eating habits. The key is eating more slowly, taking small bites and chewing your food thoroughly. Diarrhea is not uncommon during the first couple of weeks after surgery. The anesthesia often causes loose stools as can the all-liquid, post-op diet.

carbohydrates. This means some kind of protein at every meal.

Good protein sources include poultry, beef, fish, pork, eggs, cheese, beans and legumes (such as black beans or pintos), tofu and nuts. We also recommend that you take a daily liquid or chewable vitamin, something health professionals are increasingly recommending for everyone.

It takes awhile to adjust to the smaller meals that will now fill you up. After all, you are undoing a lifetime of habits that you may not even be conscious of. Here are the most important rules to remember for eating and losing weight successfully throughout your LAP-BAND® journey.

• **Eat slowly.** This is imperative. This means cutting your protein into nickel-size bites. It's better to cut the pieces too small than too large. It is easy at first to forget to eat slowly, because you have probably eaten at a quicker pace all your life. Most of us who work, for instance, are used to eating lunch on the run and think nothing of it.

But now you have to think about it. If you lapse into old habits, eat too quickly and fail to chew your food well enough, your body and your band will let you know that it's not acceptable. You'll also want to avoid distracted eating. That is, eating while driving your car, for instance, or working at your computer. Set aside 30 minutes to concentrate only on eating.

• **Chew your food well.** This means holding it in your mouth longer and chewing more than you're used to. It takes time for this to become second nature. If you find yourself forgetting and swallowing food that's not completely chewed, here's a technique we've developed to help you out: Take a small bite of food. Chew it carefully until it's in liquid form. You may have the urge swallow once or twice with the food remaining in your mouth, but don't.

Next, place your tongue on the roof of your mouth and, with your mouth closed, exhale. Then tilt your head back slightly, and allow the chewed-up food to start sliding down your throat. Then swallow. After you get more accustomed to eating with the band, you'll develop your own adaptation, which will eventually become something you do automatically.

• **Don't eat and drink at the same time.** You may think you can't learn to do this, but you can. If you drink liquids while you eat, you will be more prone to wash-through, wherein liquids carry food into the stomach by washing it past the band. When this happens, it takes more food for you to fill the pouch and set off the impulses to the brain that tell it you're full. You will

The Honeymoon: Learning How to Eat

Why can't I drink water with meals, once I'm banded?
Drinking water with your meals can lubricate the opening at the bottom of the pouch so that more food is allowed to flow or wash through. This defeats the purpose of the band, which is to limit the amount you eat.

Will I be able to drink a glass of water normally?
Yes. Only during the first three to four weeks after surgery should you restrict your liquids to a little at a time. Later, you can drink more at a sitting. But don't try to drink a full glass in a few big gulps. You can drink, but you can no longer chug. Moderation is always the key after surgery.

What about alcohol?
Alcohol is relatively high in calories and breaks down vitamins. But an occasional glass of wine or other alcoholic beverage isn't considered harmful to weight loss. Again, moderation is the key.

also feel fuller for a longer period of time if you refrain from drinking while you eat. Like learning to eat slowly and chew thoroughly, you must make a conscious effort in the beginning to establish this habit. You can drink liquids up to 30 minutes before you eat and resume 30 minutes after.

• **Consume 60 grams of protein every day.** You must get enough protein so that you don't feel hungry between meals and to provide your body with the building blocks it needs. Look at the palm of your hand. Each person needs three palms' worth a day of chicken, pork or fish, or another protein. Because everyone's palm is different, this is a good way to gauge the right amount for you. If you have difficulty eating hard protein at breakfast, have something soft, like a protein drink. When you fail to get enough protein, your body responds by holding onto weight, so you don't lose as quickly. You also experience more hunger.

• **Drink at least 48 ounces of water a day.** That's six 8-ounce glasses. More is preferable. Why? Besides keeping you hydrated, water helps to flush the toxins of weight loss out of your body. If you don't provide enough water, the toxins will exit in some other way. They might, for example, cause facial breakouts, even in people well beyond adolescence. Drinking water is best, but you can count tea and beverages like Crystal Light toward your daily water total.

• **Exercise.** Activity helps increase your metabolism. It's also an essential component of overall health. We understand that many overweight or

Once I'm banded, do I need to take vitamin supplements?

You can get all the vitamins and nutrients you need from food after you are banded because the LAP-BAND® doesn't change how your food is digested. But we concur with the many health professionals who recommend that all adults take a daily multivitamin as a nutritional safety net. Banded patients should choose liquids, chewables or Viactiv multivitamin chews because they can be more easily broken down than a pill.

What about eating out?

You'll order only a small amount of food, such as an appetizer, soup or fish. If you're with others, eat slowly, so as to finish at the same time as your companions. You might want to let the person who invited you know ahead of time that you cannot eat very much.

Also, because you cannot control how the protein is cooked, be sure to include what we call food lube in your order. This is your insurance against dry, overcooked meat. It might be a sauce that is served on the side or a bit of salad dressing, like ranch with chicken. After cutting your protein into small bites, dip the tines of your fork in the sauce, then spear a bite of food. Don't dip the food in the sauce, or you'll fill up too quickly.

obese people don't feel good enough to exercise. Maybe your feet or joints hurt, you tire easily, or you get out of breath quickly. Maybe you're self-conscious about going to a gym or other public place. But the sooner you increase your activity, the more quickly you will lose weight and feel better.

That said, everyone begins this part of the program at their own pace. Some people, like actor Dennis Burkley from Chapter 2, begin an exercise program right away. Others wait until some of their weight has come off and they start to feel more energetic. Some find it useful to substitute activity as a diversion when food is no longer the central force in their life.

However you begin, when you begin, walking is a good place to start.

• **Weigh and measure yourself regularly.** It's important to weigh yourself so that you can track progress. But you don't want to do it obsessively. We recommend getting on the scale about once a week and keeping a written record. Then, too, how your clothes fit can sometimes be a better gauge of your weight loss than actual pounds lost, which is why we also recommend measuring yourself monthly.

Sometimes you will lose a clothing size before you lose pounds, especially if you are exercising and building muscle, which weighs more than fat and burns more energy than fat. You'll want to measure your waist, chest, hips, arms,

What are stop signals?

Your body will clearly tell you when it has had enough to eat at a meal. But it will take your eyes and your mind a while to adjust to this. Sliming, a sudden surge in the production of mucous and saliva, is the body's most forceful signal to stop eating. When your pouch is full, you will feel the impulse to stop eating, as the signal from your pouch reaches your brain. This can be subtle, and you may be used to overriding it. When you are banded, you need to listen and stop when it says stop. Otherwise, you will end up spitting up or, worse, vomiting.

and thighs, as well as any other part that seems pertinent for you. Some guys, for example, will also measure their necks.

• **See your doctor on a regular basis.** We encourage patients to stay in touch. During the weight-loss phase, this means getting fills and checking in to be sure you're making progress. It also means calling the doctor's office if something doesn't seem right.

We encourage patients to become part of our after-care program, which addresses many issues that are not necessarily medical, from something as simple as finding a good protein shake to swapping stories about non-scale victories – triumphs that aren't tied to numbers, such as climbing stairs without getting winded. An after-care program is also a ready-made support

group that gives you a chance to talk to others who understand what you're going through. Not only is it helpful to know you're not alone, but you pick up insights you wouldn't get anyplace else. Plus, it's a safe environment in which to share your fears or concerns. If you feel you need more support than this offers or you are having a particularly difficult time with an emotional issue, it may be time for a counseling referral.

LAP-BAND® eating 102

Before we get into the finer points about eating banded, we want to give a few more details about spitting up.

Very simply, when you put something in your stomach pouch that's not chewed well enough to pass through the opening between the pouch and your stomach, your body spits it back up.

This is different from vomiting because the food hasn't had the chance to mix with your gastric juices. So it isn't unpleasant in the way vomiting is. The chewed food just comes back up. Even though it's not unpleasant, one of your goals should be to chew your food well enough on a consistent basis so that spitting up occurs less than once a week. Some people also refer to this as a productive burp, or PB.

We also said that no one would give you a list of what you can eat and drink vs. what you can't. **There is one exception: Don't drink carbonated beverages.** Carbonation is not good for the band. It can cause pain and, over the long run, stretch your pouch.

There are also some foods that you may find more difficult to eat with your band. You'll want to experiment to see what's true for you. Some people have to work up slowly to beef, for instance, and find that fish and chicken are easier to manage.

Some people never really get comfortable with tough or well-done beef. This can even vary in an individual from one fill to another because you're changing the size of the opening between your pouch and your stomach. The following tips build on the basics and will help you fine-tune your eating habits for maximum comfort and weight loss.

• Eat soft or liquid foods that are high in calories only in moderation. Because these slide easily past the band, eating too much of them will sabotage and slow your weight loss. Some examples are cream soups, mashed potatoes, ice cream, milkshakes, guacamole, pudding, mousse, whipped cream, and chocolate.

• There are a few foods you might choose to avoid simply because they pose an extra challenge with the band. With soft white bread, for example, the gluten mixes with your saliva, and the bread swells in your stomach.

The Honeymoon: Learning How to Eat

Is it true that the LAP-BAND® seems tighter in the morning?

Yes, this is a fairly common feeling, especially if your band is tight or you've just had it adjusted. Over the course of the day, the water content in your body changes, and this may also cause the band to feel tighter at times. Some women have also noticed that the band feels tighter during their periods.

What is slippage?

Slippage occurs when a part of the stomach works its way up (slips) through the band and causes the small pouch to become enlarged. The violent contractions of vomiting can cause this, but it can also happen on its own. In Dr. Jayaseelan's practice, we have seen this in about 10 percent of patients. When it does happen, the band must be repositioned surgically.

Many patients decide to forego white bread. For some patients, something similar happens with pasta, as well as dried fruits, which can expand and get lodged in the small opening of the stomach pouch. You may decide it's just not worth it to try and eat some of these foods. With fibrous or stringy vegetables as well as fruits with edible skins, you also may wish to take it more slowly.

But it's a myth that people who are banded can't eat such foods, which include asparagus, pineapple, rhubarb, corn, popcorn, broccoli, grapes, and skin-on apples and pears. Rather than giving them up, be smart about how you prepare them. Stringy vegetables, for example, usually need to be well-cooked to overcooked. And if you like asparagus, you might find it easier to eat only the tips of the spears after you're banded.

If you like raw apples and pears, they go down easier if you peel them, or even cook them. And some people find that grapes are fine as long as they are frozen. Experiment and be creative to find out what works for you.

• **Don't wait until you're famished to eat.** This sometimes results in what we call First Bite Syndrome. You wait too long, you forget that you're banded, and you gobble down the first few bites, chewing haphazardly, as instinct takes over. This is a subconscious move. It's what we all did as unbanded people, and it's a natural reaction to being very hungry: You're trying to quickly get the message to your brain and stomach that food is on the way.

But this is precisely the kind of behavior that will cause problems with the band. Food that's not thoroughly chewed is likely to get stuck. If that happens, you may spit up. If you do find yourself in a situation where you're

Tips for getting enough protein
Here are some ways to help you get the protein you need each day:

- *Quaker Oats weight-control oatmeal. It has 7 grams of protein per serving, and if you add milk, that increases the protein.*
- *Lunch-meat roll-ups. A lot of lunch meats are soft and easy to chew. Eat them plain, or add a little mayonnaise or mustard for flavor, roll them up and enjoy. Cheese makes a good addition, too.*

- *Cheese. Small bites can satisfy quickly, and you get a calcium bonus.*
- *Protein bars. They're a good way to make the afternoon hungries go away.*
- *Protein drinks. Check out the chart on Page 124 showing the results of our after-care group protein-drink taste test.*
- *Protein water. This is flavored water to which protein has been added.*

extremely hungry, force yourself to take a moment and cut your protein, such as a half chicken breast, in half. Then cut half of that into tiny bites. Eat tiny bites first. Then continue with the rest of the meal. This will help prevent you from taking too large a bite initially and getting stuck.

• **Don't drink your calories.** Fruit drinks and juices, sports drinks such as Gatorade, even milk can sabotage your weight loss. Learn to drink water or no-calorie beverages such as Crystal Light, coffee and tea.

Simultaneously with the honeymoon, as we've suggested, you will begin dealing in earnest with your divorce from food. Many of our patients find this to be the most difficult challenge of the LAP-BAND® journey. Some people are genuinely surprised to discover how much they have been eating before becoming banded, how much time food has taken up in their lives, and how difficult it is to give up. This was the case for Scott Gaines, who found that breaking up really was hard to do. His story leads off the next chapter.

Never-Fail Marinated Chicken or Pork

This method keeps the meat moist and flavorful and easy to chew.

Start with **3 or 4 boneless, skinless chicken-breast halves** (or 3 or 4 slices of pork tenderloin) about the size of a deck of cards. Trim away any fat. Season both sides with **Knorr all-purpose seasoning for meat** and **Italian seasoning blend**. Place the meat in a plastic zip-top bag with ¼ **cup olive oil.** Squeeze as much air out of the bag as you can and seal it tightly.

Wrap the bag in a kitchen towel, and, using a meat mallet or rolling pin, beat the chicken or pork on both sides to tenderize it. Allow the meat to come to room temperature as it marinates for 30 minutes. Note: If you do not plan to cook it immediately, marinate it in the refrigerator, then bring it out in time to warm to room temperature. Cooking the meat at room temperature helps make it tender.

Heat a skillet over medium heat, and empty contents of bag into it. Sear meat on both sides, then reduce heat, cover and cook on low just until it is tender and cooked through. Don't overcook, or the texture will be rubbery. Add salt to taste. Serve with jarred marinara sauce and a dusting of Parmesan cheese, if desired. Makes 4 entrée-size servings or 8 to 10 banded servings.

Variations:

Greek: Add 1 tablespoon lemon juice and substitute Greek oregano for the Italian blend.

Southwestern: Add 1 tablespoon lime juice and substitute chile powder for Italian blend.

French: Substitute herbes de Provence for the Italian blend.

Asian: Use roasted sesame oil instead of olive oil, omit the seasoning blend, and add 1 teaspoon soy sauce, 2 teaspoons rice vinegar and 1 teaspoon grated fresh ginger.

Never-Fail Moist Fish

Microwave poaching is easy and seals in juices.

Place a **fish fillet**, such as salmon, halibut, mahi mahi, or orange roughy, about the size of a deck of cards, skin-side-down, in a small, microwave-proof dish.

In a small bowl, mix together **2 tablespoons lemon juice, 1 teaspoon soy sauce, 1 tablespoon finely chopped shallots** or **sweet onion** (optional), and **$1/4$ cup water**.

Pour this over the fish. Add a **pat of butter** or **drizzle of olive oil** on top. Cover loosely with plastic wrap and microwave on High (100 percent power) for 2 minutes. Test fish for doneness: It should separate easily with a fork. Or, push on the surface of the fish with your finger. If it gives only a little, it's done. If it gives a lot or feels mushy, microwave a minute more.

Let stand at least 30 seconds before removing plastic wrap. Remove the skin before serving. Spoon a little of the cooking juices over the top, if desired. Add **salt** and **pepper** to taste. Makes 1 banded serving.

Easy Sauce: Mix together **2 tablespoons of good quality mayonnaise** with **1 teaspoon chopped, rinsed capers**.

Variations:

You can substitute chopped leeks (rinsed and cleaned, white portion only) for the shallots or onions. You can also add your favorite seasoning mix, such as Italian seasoning, Cajun seasoning or one of the Mrs. Dash blends.

Tilapia Meuniere

Mix together **1 cup milk** and **1 egg**. Soak **1 pound tilapia fillets** (about 4 to 6) in the milk-egg mixture for an hour. *(Note: You can skip that step if you're in a hurry, but the fish won't be as tender.)*

In a mixing bowl, combine **1 cup flour, 2 teaspoons Knorr Swiss Aromat Seasoning for Meat, 1 teaspoon salt, 1 teaspoon Lawry's Lemon-Pepper** and **1 tablespoon dried parsley flakes**. Shake excess liquid off of fillets and lightly coat each one with the seasoned flour.

In a skillet over medium heat, melt ¹/₂ **cup butter** with ¹/₄ **cup olive oil, 2 cloves garlic** slightly mashed with a fork and **3 tablespoons lemon juice**. Heat until bubbly. Remove garlic.

Increase heat to medium-high. Add fillets and cook 4 to 5 minutes, turning once. They will be golden. Serve with pan juices and **lemon wedges**. Makes 4 to 6 entrée-size servings or 10 to 12 banded servings.

Slow Cooker Pot Roast

This produces a tender pot roast – and lots of it. Makes sure you have friends and family to share. Or, package meal-sized portions in zip-top freezer bags and freeze for future use.

Trim the fat off a **3- to 4-pound top round or chuck roast**. Cut it into about 6 pieces. Place the meat in the slow cooker. Add **1 (11-ounce) can condensed cream of mushroom soup, 1 medium onion** cut in large dice, and **8 ounces of sliced fresh mushrooms**. Cover and cook on Low for 8 to 10 hours, or until very tender.

Remove beef and veggies to a platter. Skim any excess fat from the remaining juices, if needed.

Meanwhile, melt **1 tablespoon butter** in a medium saucepan over medium-high heat. Add **2 tablespoons of flour**. Cook, stirring, until butter-flour mixture turns light brown. Add the juices from the slow cooker, and continue cooking till thickened. Add **salt** and **pepper** to taste. Serve on the side or over the pot roast. Makes 4 to 6 normal entrée-size servings, or 10 to 12 banded servings.

Slow Cooker Shredded Beef

Trim excess fat from a **4- to 5-pound chuck roast**. Mix together **1 teaspoon onion powder, 1 teaspoon garlic powder, $^1/_2$ teaspoon salt**, and $^1/_4$ **teaspoon black pepper**. Press the mixture into the roast.

Place the roast in 4 $^1/_2$ quart slow cooker. Pour **1 (14-ounce) can fat-free beef broth** around the roast, being careful not to get it on the roast (so that the seasonings aren't washed off). Add 1 large onion, sliced into rings. Cook on low for 8 to 10 hours.

Remove beef from cooker and, using 2 forks, carefully shred the beef. Add the beef back into the pot with the cooking liquid, and stir well. Makes about 8 cups. Add your favorite barbecue sauce for zip. To save some for later, freeze in 1-cup batches in freezer zip-top bags, making sure to squeeze out as much air as possible. The beef will keep for several months.

Paige's Pork Chops

Season both sides of **4 pork chops** (bone-in or butterflied) with **garlic salt** and **pepper**. Dredge the chops in flour. Heat **2 tablespoons olive oil** in a skillet over medium heat, and cook the pork chops just until they are done. The salt helps the pork chops stay juicy. Makes 4 entrée-size servings or 8 to 10 banded servings.

Sweet Potato Fries

Preheat oven to 400° F. Peel and cut **5 sweet potatoes** into 1x5-inch sticks. Line a baking sheet with foil. Set aside. Place the sweet potato fries in a bowl with $^1/_4$ **cup olive oil** and toss to coat.

Arrange on the prepared baking sheet and bake until crisp and golden, shaking the pan occasionally, about 45 minutes. While the potatoes bake, combine **2 teaspoons sea salt** and $^1/_2$ **teaspoon freshly ground black pepper** in a small bowl.

Remove sweet potato fries from oven, sprinkle with salt/pepper mixture and serve. You may also add dried herbs of your choice. Makes 4 to 6 normal servings or 8 to 12 banded servings.

Faux Mashed Potatoes

Simmer **4 cups cauliflower florets** in **salted water** to cover until tender, but not mushy. Drain. Microwave **2 tablespoons butter** and $1/8$ **cup half-and-half** (or whole milk) long enough to melt the butter. Place butter, milk and florets in a blender; puree until smooth.

You may have to do this in batches. Or, mash by hand with a potato masher or whisk until most of the lumps are gone. Add **pepper** to taste, if desired. Adjust seasonings. Makes 4 normal servings or 8 to 12 banded servings.

Fresh Spinach

Use **baby spinach**, which is sold bagged and washed. After steaming it until it's tender, squeeze some of the water out, add about **1 tablespoon olive oil** or to taste, $1/8$ **teaspoon garlic powder**, and **salt** to taste. Serve immediately. One bag makes 1 to 2 normal servings or 3 to 4 banded servings.

Leftover spinach idea:
Make a single, **small-egg omelet**, and fold it over the warmed, leftover cooked spinach plus some sour cream or plain yogurt. Add salt to taste.

Food prep tips

A-peeling fruit: Peel the skin off fruits such as apples, pears, and peaches to make them go down more easily.

Grapes that go down easy: If grapes are problematic to get down for you, try freezing them before you eat them.

Check out this cookbook: *Eating Well After Weight-Loss Surgery*
By Patt Levine and Michele Bontempo-Saray (Marlowe & Co., $16.95)

Scott: What you don't know can hurt you

Before my LAP-BAND® procedure

After my LAP-BAND® procedure

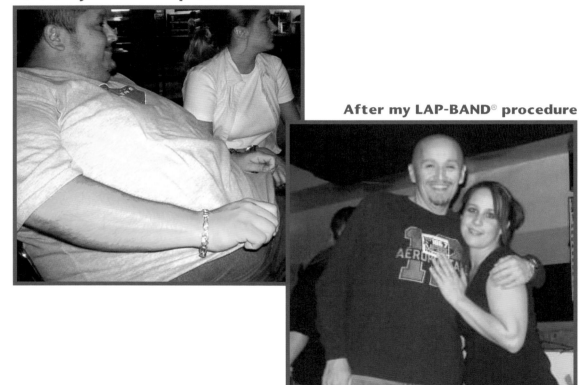

Chapter 6 | The Divorce: Your New Relationship with Food

Scott Gaines was not prepared for the shocker that awaited once he was banded: "I didn't realize how much of a food addiction I really had," says the radio personality from Rochester Hills, Mich. Then again, Scott also didn't realize how much weight he had gained over a decade. At his heaviest, he weighed 376 pounds and stood 6 feet tall. "It didn't bother me," he says. "I didn't think about it." He'd always tended to be chubby, he says, but all through high school and college, he'd been athletic and so managed to keep his weight under control. After graduation was a different story. "I started working in radio, started working nights," he says. "I still had the same appetite, but I wasn't working out. After about 10 years, I'd put that much weight on."

Just how big he'd become hit home only when he was getting ready for his honeymoon cruise. One of the nights, there was to be a dress-up dinner. "I needed some slacks," he says, "and I believe I had to have a 67-inch waist." That got his attention. Meanwhile, a friend at the radio station where he worked had had LAP-BAND® surgery, and Scott was impressed with how good she looked. "I started looking for my own doctor."

But after getting banded in August 2004, Scott had to confront and do battle with the food addiction he didn't know he had. "I didn't

realize how bad my habits were. Not completely chewing, and eating too fast. Eating in large quantity. The band lets you know. If you eat too big of a bite, you'll spit it back up. I wouldn't call that a drawback. That's what I consider a safety mechanism."

Boosting physical activity wasn't hard for Scott, who drew on his past athletic experience. But it did take time. "I started out slow, really slow. My wife and I would walk real slow." Eventually, he worked up to running. Now he has a treadmill and weights at home.

Scott says that Dr. Jayaseelan, who was his

surgeon, told him that he could tell from the muscles under his fat that he had been an athlete at one time. "He said, 'We'll get you back down to where you'll recognize that guy again. He's in there.'" Five years later, at 185 pounds, Scott has reclaimed that guy.

Part of Scott's food divorce included a period of anger about his food addiction. "I never knew how much of an addiction I had," he says. "I think with that, it's like alcoholism or drug addiction. It never truly goes away."

Instead, he says he's found ways to manage it. "I've done everything I can to be successful. I followed the rules. I've done this for five years now, and I think this is what normal is." He adds: "I don't regret a minute of it. I only wish I'd done it sooner."

※

During the honeymoon period, you also begin your divorce from food in earnest. One of the first signs is often the experience of something we call Head Hunger: This is when your head tells you that you need to eat despite what your body says. Even though you may not be physically hungry, you pick up on external cues and mental signals that say you should be.

Here's an example: You find yourself staring into the refrigerator, certain that you need food. Your mind says, "It's noon. Time to eat. I always eat at noon." But when you pay close attention, you find that you're not actually hungry. After a while, when these urges come over you, you'll learn to ask, "Am I really hungry? Or, is this a habit I'm carrying over from the old me?"

Here's another example: Maybe you're stressing over something and you really want that pint of Häagen-Dazs, which you've relied on for comfort in the past. You get it out of the freezer, pop the lid, and dig in. But after only a few bites, you find that you can't eat any more because you're full.

Your head says you've got to have it, but your new band says, "No, you don't." You will learn to ask appropriate questions: "Am I really hungry? Or, am I experiencing an uncomfortable feeling that makes me want to eat?"

It takes awhile to manage feelings like stress and anger differently, especially if food has been a coping strategy in your former life. Eventually, when Head Hunger hits, you'll be able to ask, "Why am I really running to the kitchen? What am I experiencing or thinking that makes me want to do this?" This won't happen in a snap, but you will learn.

As you adjust to the band, you also may be mortified by how much of your former life was consumed by food. You may be surprised at how much time and energy you invested in eating. You may become angry or disgusted with yourself when you start confronting just how high a priority food got in your former life.

Perhaps you loved food more than you loved your pet, or you routinely chose eating by yourself at home instead of a night out with friends or family. As a consequence, it's fairly common to become irritable at some point during this period. You might yell at your spouse for no reason or become short-tempered with your children.

Be assured that this is temporary and normal; the irritability is displaced anger. You're being forced to come to grips with how much power food has had over you.

At the same time, you're being forced to give up your old, familiar ways. You're frustrated that you can't turn to your usual source of comfort. It's a lot like grieving. Even though getting banded was voluntary and you are committed to losing the weight, you've lost something that was important to you.

There are other reasons why you might feel irritable during the divorce period. It's not unusual for people to become grumpy after their first fill. You've been working hard at re-learning how to eat, how to chew and how to listen to your body, and you suddenly get impatient for it to work faster.

It's also beginning to sink in that you might actually lose weight this time and that this weight-loss experience won't end like all the diets you've tried. You may feel anxious that you're not losing as much weight as you should. Or worse, that you're gaining weight.

Your emotions about this may push and pull you in two directions at once. That's why during the first six weeks, we recommend that you keep your expectations modest: Assume you won't lose much weight, if any. That way, anything you do lose is a bonus.

What do you do now?

When you have spent so much of your time thinking about food, touching food, dealing with food and shopping for food, you have to find something else to do when this is taken away. This is a pivotal moment in your journey. You literally have to find a new activity to keep your

Tick, tick, tick

Years ago, when I was told I had to have my gallbladder removed, I was scared and depressed. I had never had surgery before. I was in pain, and I thought the pain would never stop. I felt like I was going to feel that way forever.

That's when my dad sat me down and said, "Tick, tick, tick." I had no idea what I was supposed to get from this. "Time passes very quickly," he explained gently. "By tomorrow at this time, the surgery will be over. A week from now, you'll be home and on the mend. A month from now, and you'll be back at work. In six months, all you'll have to remember the surgery by is a scar. Life will go on."

It took me a while to understand what he meant, but he was right. Time does pass. And whatever you're feeling or going through now will change. I have learned to use those three little words to get me through everything from school exams to a broken heart.

When I went for my LAP-BAND® surgery, I thought, "Tick, tick, tick. A week from now, I will be home and healing."

For those times on the banded journey when I had to do something I didn't want to do, I thought, "Tick, tick, tick."

When relationships didn't work out, the same three words got me through the pain and sadness. When I wanted to eat my way through anger, those three words kept me from overindulging.

When we go through the weight-loss process with the band, a lot of us confront uncomfortable feelings. These may be the same feelings that we avoided in the first place by eating. Some may be quite painful. Tick, tick, tick. Time will pass. The situation will change.

When people are sitting on the fence about getting the surgery, I tell them that six months from now, they will be 30 to 60 pounds slimmer. Time will pass quickly. If they don't have the surgery, they could be 10 pounds heavier by then.

After banding, when you're sore: Tick, tick, tick. Maybe you have some slippage, or have to have fluid removed: Tick, tick, tick. Maybe you're down on yourself for making a bad food choice: Tick, tick, tick.

Make it your mantra. When you're sitting in traffic, remember that in an hour, it will be in the past. If you're going through a tough time with your significant other: Tick, tick, tick. If you have no significant other: Tick, tick, tick.

My father was right. Time does pass quickly, and things do change and get better. It has been several years since my father died, but his words of wisdom have helped shape my life. When things get hard, I remember what he said. I survive. I learn. I live.

- Cynthia Jones O'Kelly

The Divorce: Your New Relationship with Food

hands busy and your mind occupied because spending so much time with food is no longer an option.

Instead of dwelling too much on what you have lost, recognize it for what it is and concentrate on the adventure of discovering what activities you'll choose to take its place.

Some people get more involved with their children's or grandchildren's activities. Some develop new hobbies, such as painting, ceramics, woodworking or needlepoint. Some begin furiously reorganizing closets, attics, garages, or family albums.

Others try to escape into their computer or TV. But be warned: This option doesn't work in the long run because you need to *do* something with your hands.

Passively watching TV or sitting at a keyboard won't be enough. So the more you can nudge yourself toward activities that get you moving and doing in the first place, the better.

Then, too, this is the time when a lot of people learn to channel their energy into sports - the active kind - or some new activity, such as a daily walk.

The point is, you can no longer fixate on food. Figuratively speaking, food as you have known it has packed its bags and left the room. You can't go back. You must go forward.

Another aspect of this transition is learning to look at meals differently. Up to this point, you have been accustomed to a certain amount of food filling you up at a meal. This isn't even conscious: You sit down, fill your plate and eat without thinking.

You may find yourself going into a restaurant and ordering for the "old" you because it will still feel like you need a certain amount of food to satisfy your hunger. Slowly, as your refrigerator becomes a sea of to-go cartons full of food you bring home, you'll learn to order differently. You also may need to just lighten up and accept that your eyes will be bigger than your stomach for a while.

Eventually it will sink in that, no matter how hungry you feel, you should order less than you think you want. You'll figure out that you can't order an appetizer, a salad and an entrée like you used to, because you'll be full after the salad.

The new you will get along very nicely on an appetizer and nothing more. Or, if you must have an entrée, divide it with someone. You just won't be able to eat the amount of food you used to.

Stop before you slime

If First Bite Syndrome means gobbling food too fast when you're hungry, Last Bite Syndrome means wanting to eat One Last Bite, even though your body and your band suddenly tell you that you're finished.

Signals that it's time to stop eating take several forms. Some people experience port pain, shoulder pain, hiccups, burping, watering eyes, passing gas or runny noses. It is important to identify your stop signal and pay attention to it.

Don't be surprised when you sometimes resist this feeling like a rebellious child, informing your band that you weren't given any notice that that was the Last Bite. Inside your head, you may argue with your band as you try to convince it to let you have a real Last Bite that you can savor. This is why you will sometimes see floating forks when banded folk eat.

They are having this inner conversation with their band. The forks of experienced bandsters finally will make it back down to their plate. Others will tempt fate and press forward with that Last Bite, even though the band is clearly saying "no." Then you will see them excuse themselves to go to the restroom, because they will need to spit up.

Their bodies will begin to overproduce saliva and mucous in a misguided attempt to get that last, forbidden bite down. This is sliming in action. It's also worth pointing out that spitting up is not a stop signal. It's a sign that you have gone past the point of fullness and are now stretching your pouch and esophagus. When the band says you're full, no matter what's on your plate or what you think you deserve, **you are full**.

If you have difficulty mastering the recognition of your stop signal, try this: When you sit down at the table, eat for 20 minutes. Then stop and do something else for 10 minutes. Only if you are still hungry go back and eat more. In most cases, you will notice that you are full and desire no more food. This should occur after you've had an amount of food equal to the size of your palm, or about $1/2$ to 1 cup.

This is also a good time to remind yourself that losing weight with the LAP-BAND® is not a race. It's not about who loses the fastest. Your desired weight loss will come with time, with patience, and with adherence to the rules for eating and living differently. The weight will come off slowly which, among other things, gives your body time to adjust. And you won't be starving your body of nutrients during the process.

By the three-month mark, you should start having a fairly good idea of what foods work for you with the band. For instance, you should be able to eat most veggies by now. You also may have come to the conclusion that foods like lettuce take up too much space in return for too little nutritive value. You probably have started prioritizing what you eat.

And although you're cleared to eat hard protein by now, you may find that you still want to go slowly and ease into these foods. Fish, whose flesh is moist and less dense than some protein foods, is usually a good choice. When you eat chicken or pork, you'll want them to be juicy or have a little sauce. For beef, you'll probably want to start with tenderloin or something like pot roast that has been cooked to extreme tenderness. Beef stew, on the other hand, with its tougher chunks of meat, might spell trouble even for an advanced bandster.

By the end of the fourth month, it should be clear that the divorce is final, and your new, lifelong marriage to band has begun.

You're still in for some fascinating, interesting and surprising times to come – like what happens when you are no longer invisible and people begin to see you. When Mitchell Robinson moved to go to culinary school halfway through his LAP-BAND® journey, classmates were fascinated by his before photos. They had never known him at his heaviest weight – and got to watch him achieve his goal weight. His story leads off the next chapter.

Getting out of your comfort zone

Remember when you were a kid and got a big gift during a holiday, and the box it came in turned out to be more fun than the gift? You could make it be a fort, a house, a castle, or whatever you could dream up. But regardless of what you called it, you felt safe inside those cardboard walls.

One of my favorite games with a box was to hide from imaginary bad guys. I was safe inside my box. No bogeyman could penetrate my box. As I grew up, I built a figurative box around myself that held that same feeling of safety.

As I got fatter and fatter, this imaginary box took on greater importance. And in time it became my comfort zone. It was lovely inside my box, where I had all the comforts I needed: food, bed, TV, bathroom. I could get things delivered. It even got to the point where I tried to be home to my box after work by a certain hour.

At times, it was lonely. But that was preferable to the uncertainties of being outside it. No worry at mealtime that I wouldn't fit into a booth. No fear that I'd break a chair. With catalogs and online, I could avoid snotty salespeople who would look down on me because of my size. And my car was like my portable comfort zone as well as escape pod, so I could make a getaway, if need be.

When I was at my heaviest – 340 pounds on a 5-foot-1-inch frame – my best friend ran off to Hawaii to get married. I always guessed that I was part of the reason. She was gorgeous, and I would not have looked attractive coming down the aisle right before her. She and her new husband did hold a reception when they got back, and I noticed that she did not introduce me to any of the single men there. By shunning me – that was my perception – my friend drove me deeper into my box.

As I lost weight, part of the process was testing the world outside my box. I was terrified, but I began slowly. I started going back to church. I accepted some of the few invitations that were extended to me.

There have been times when I have walked into a party and known no one but the hostess and felt scared to death. One time, I shared this with the first person I met at the party, and do you know what she did? She introduced me to everyone there she knew. I made new friends, and my comfort zone expanded.

As you lose weight, you have to make a conscious effort to break out of your box. You may be surprised to discover that we're all the same - fat, thin, black, white, short, tall. We all get scared, and we all get lonely.

Think about your box. What does it look like outside? What does it look like inside? The next time someone tries to coax you out of your box, go for it. Take a chance. Paint that picture. Go to that party. Stay out past 10.

Do something, anything, to move yourself forward in life each day. You may hit a wall - heck, I still do. But I keep getting right back up, grabbing that hammer and chisel, and working on my next prison break. Don't let your box become your jail.

- Cynthia Jones O'Kelly

The Divorce: Your New Relationship with Food

Mitchell: Building on success

Before my LAP-BAND® procedure

After my LAP-BAND® procedure

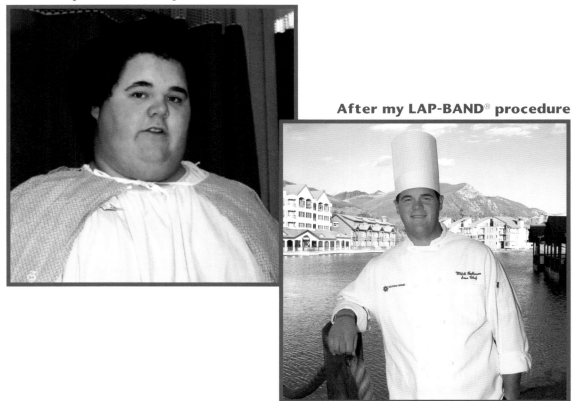

Before Mitchell Robinson ever moved to Silverthorne, Colo., he and his friends would vacation there to ski. Except that, in 2002, Mitchell couldn't ski with them: "We couldn't find a ski boot to fit around my calf," he says. So while his friends skied, Mitchell, who carried 392 pounds on a 6-foot frame, stayed in the condo his parents owned or went snowmobiling.

But when Mitchell moved to Silverthorne, Colo., three and a half years ago to go to culinary school, it was a different story. By then, he had already lost 100 pounds with his LAP-BAND®, which he got after seeing his mother's success with hers.

"I got it in March 2004," he says, and moved to Silverthorne, which is west of Denver, the following December. His classmates noticed that he didn't eat a lot and asked why. "They were pretty impressed when I told them my story," he says. "They wanted to see pictures from before." They were fascinated by what he had looked like – and how different he looked after moving to Colorado.

You might think that culinary school would be one temptation after another for a banded person. But, as Mitchell explains, he got a fill right before moving that was a little on the tight side, and when he was at school in the kitchen, "I took little bites of everything. I learned to deal with it. If something tastes good, I just take one bite. I can't eat a big portion."

Not only that, where he lives has helped him drop another 100 pounds for 200 total. "When I first got the band, I was not exercising at all. Then I moved up here, and exercise goes hand-in-hand. I ski 70 days out of the season. In the summer, I ride my mountain bike three or four times a week. I also hike and do all kinds of stuff outside."

The altitude also gives his weight loss a boost, he says. "I live so high altitude-wise that you kind of lose your appetite. I'm living at 10,000 feet. When I first got here, I was working at 12,000. Just running upstairs would get a normal person winded."

As for those ski boots, "I rented last season because I found a boot that fit. That was a victory.

"Now, I don't have to special-order boots or ski clothes," he adds. "I can go into any store and get whatever I want."

He likes Colorado so much that he decided to stay after he graduated in May. Today he lives in Montezuma, Colo., and is a sous chef at a major ski resort nearby.

"I pretty much eat what I want now," *he says. His band was unfilled a couple* *years ago, he adds, and that, along with his Rocky Mountain lifestyle, is enough restriction to keep his weight stable.*

You will get your first fill about six weeks after your LAP-BAND® surgery, after your body has had time to heal. At your first follow-up appointment after surgery, you and your doctor will decide when to schedule this.

The LAP-BAND® isn't inflated at the time of surgery because the operation itself, as with any operation, will cause swelling,

What is a fill, or adjustment?

Once the LAP-BAND® is in place and you are past the healing process, you will schedule a visit with your doctor for your first fill. Generally, these are not performed before five to six weeks after your surgery. The fill takes only a few minutes. First, your doctor will locate the port and give you an injection to deaden the skin. Then he will use a different needle filled with saline solution to gently inflate the LAP-BAND®. On occasion, he may deflate it, if it feels too restrictive or for other reasons.

The fill, or adjustment, allows you to adjust your food consumption rate. With the local anesthetic on your skin above the port, the procedure is virtually painless. Most patients need four to six fills the first year. When and how much to fill will be determined by your weight loss, the amount of food that you can comfortably eat, your exercise regimen, and other health issues, as well as the amount of fluid already in the band. We also recommend that adjustments be performed using an X-ray, which allows the doctor to watch what is happening inside your body, or a sonogram, which allows the doctor to see your port clearly.

How many LAP-BAND® fills or adjustments will I need?

The number can't be determined in advance of surgery because every patient is different. We typically see patients getting four to six fills the first year. A few patients need only one. Some require more. Basically, patients need adjustments when their restriction decreases or their weight-loss stops. You will also require fills because, as you lose weight, the fat around your stomach as well as your stomach itself, shrinks.

in this case around your stomach and the port area. The swelling where the band is placed around the stomach will contribute to an initial feeling of restriction that may make you feel less hungry. But as your body adjusts to the presence of the band, the swelling decreases and you will notice that you're gradually becoming hungrier and consuming more.

When your stomach is no longer swollen and you're definitely experiencing hunger, it's time to fill your band. But because everyone is different, this may not occur at exactly six weeks. You may continue to feel the kind of restriction that slows hunger for several more weeks.

And if that's the case, there's no reason to rush in for a fill. The point of the fill is to give you the right amount of restriction in the band, and if you're already experiencing plenty of restriction, there's no reason to change it. Eventually, though, you'll be ready for a fill.

Here's what you can expect at your first fill appointment. We're going to tell you how we do this in Dr. Jayaseelan's practice, although it may differ some with your surgeon. First, we ask you not to eat anything for four hours before arriving. We ask you not to drink anything for one hour before your appointment. This is so we can get a good look at what happens after we add the saline solution to ensure that your restriction is just right.

We tend to be conservative with the first fill. We want to make sure that you feel the restriction, but at the same time, we want to see how your body is going to react to it.

When your name is called, you'll be ushered to an examination room where a medical assistant will check your vital signs and weigh you. Then you'll go to the X-ray room. You'll lie down on a table and lift your shirt to expose your tummy where the port is.

Are adjustments (fills) covered by health insurance?

You or your doctor will have to verify your benefits to ensure that you have coverage for the procedure. For the most part, patients with coverage are able to get their adjustments for the price of an office visit co-pay. If your health insurance does not cover band adjustments, you will need to arrange payment for these yourself. Arrangements vary from surgeon to surgeon, but you should be able to work this out well in advance of your surgery.

The medical assistant will gently feel your skin to locate the port and scrub the area with Betadine or a similar antimicrobial solution. Then the doctor (or nurse practitioner) will give you a brief injection at the site to deaden the skin. This is the only thing that will hurt, and it will feel like a pinch.

Sometimes, people are more afraid of the fill procedure, with its needles, than the original surgery. If that describes you, rest assured that once you've had this done a few times, it will be easy. After the skin has been deadened, we use the X-ray to show us where to insert the fill needle into the port.

Some surgeons elect not to anchor the port to the muscle with stitches. But it is our experience that locating the port for fills after surgery is much easier when it is in a secured spot.

The doctor will you talk to you about what kind of restriction you've been feeling and how it feels when, using a hypodermic needle, he begins to inject saline solution into the band.

Generally, it takes only a few minutes, because the band is small and doesn't require a lot to inflate. When you and the doctor think it's right, he'll ask you to drink about an ounce of thin liquid barium (not the thick stuff of an upper gastrointestinal series). Then, using the fluoroscope, he'll watch - and often, you can, too - as the liquid comes down into your stomach and moves through the band. He can instantly tell if the opening is large enough or restricted enough.

He'll also monitor what you're experiencing. You may be surprised at how small the opening is between the pouch and the main part of the stomach.

Once you see this, you'll understand why it's so important to chew your food thoroughly. Although it is possible and entirely medically safe for a doctor to perform the fill without an X-ray, we prefer this technique precisely because of what happened to Mitchell.

Using it allows the doctor to see exactly what's going on inside you at the band site. The whole process takes about five minutes.

Once the doctor is satisfied with your fill, he'll remove the needle. The assistant will wash off the Betadine, put a bandage over the injection site and give you a cup of water to sip. You'll take it with you to the waiting room and spend about 10 or 15 minutes making sure you can easily drink. If the water moves through comfortably and you are satisfied with how you feel, you'll be on your way.

When the fill feels tight

As you sit in the waiting room sipping your water after your fill, you should be able to tell fairly quickly if the fill is working for you.

If you have difficulty getting the water down, or feel like you're going to spit up, the doctor will bring you back into the X-ray room and repeat the fill steps, this time removing a bit of the saline solution. Sometimes it's only a tiny amount, like 0.25ml.

Never hesitate to bring your discomfort to the attention of the nurse or medical assistant. The doctor wants you to leave the office feeling good about your fill.

There are other instances in which the band may feel tight. Many patients report that their band feels tighter in the morning when they first wake up.

We also have reports of the band feeling tighter during illness.

Sometimes, this is due to a mucous plug, which can accumulate in the opening when you lie flat for long periods of time, or because you have an illness, such as a

Do I need to be concerned with long-term follow-up care or adjustments?

Definitely, yes. This is the most important part of the whole process. This helps ensure that the procedure will be a success. Regular follow-up visits with your doctor are necessary to track your weight loss and to make any band adjustments. If the surgeon who performs your operation will not be providing fills or follow-up care for you, you should determine before your surgery with whom and where your follow-up will be done.

cold. If that's the case, here's a way to loosen the plug: When you first get up, drink something warm and slightly acidic, such as hot water or tea with lemon in it. Avoid anything cold or creamy, such as milk.

Sometimes a band feels tight because of a stress reaction. Just as an unbanded person might get an upset stomach, banded people sometimes experience stress through their stomach.

Only for bandsters, it may feel like band tightness. Some women say their band feels tighter during their period, and a small number of people have tight bands in the evening. Unless your band is chronically tight, which might be the signal that it needs adjustment, occasional feelings of tightness are just part of the journey.

After each fill

Once again, you'll be asked to stick to a liquid diet for seven days while your stomach adjusts. For the first 24 to 48 hours, we suggest that patients stick with thin, warm or room temperature liquids. The warmth will help decrease any swelling around the stomach. You'll want to avoid extremely cold liquids during this time.

For the remainder of the seven days, you'll drink three to four protein drinks a day plus permitted fluids. Then, at the end of the seven days, you'll begin re-introducing solid foods just as you did right after the surgery. You'll want to experiment, just as you did during the healing process. What goes down and how easily may change from fill to fill. So go slowly. Chew thoroughly. Get acquainted with the restriction.

If you find that you're spitting up a lot, slow down and chew even more thoroughly. Be patient with yourself and your band. But repeated spitting up or vomiting is not normal.

If you are spitting up regularly, this means one of three things: Your band is

What is the perfect fill?

We have created what we call the Goldilocks rule of restriction: The band should not be too loose or too tight. It should be just right. Although the fills in our practice are done under fluoroscopy to see what type of restriction the patient is getting, your tummy can still seize up or completely relax shortly after a fill. This is why we ask patients to remain at the office a few minutes afterward to drink a cup of water. This way, the patient knows that he or she can easily get liquids down before leaving the office.

Is something wrong if I don't feel any restriction after my first fill?

Your first fill is usually on the conservative side because you are once again irritating your stomach by tightening the band. In our experience, it is rare to lose a lot of weight after the first fill. But about 90 percent of patients feel good restriction after the second or third fill. Although you are eager to lose weight, it's important to go slowly and to give your body time to adjust to the changes you're imposing. It helps to think of banding as a process, rather than a event.

Do I have to be careful with the access port just beneath my skin?

There are no restrictions based on the port, although you probably would not want someone to hit you there. It is placed under the skin on the abdominal muscle wall, and once the incisions heal, it should not cause discomfort or limit any physical exercise. The only sensation you may experience with the port occurs when you go for adjustments. Any persistent discomfort is a signal to talk to your doctor.

too tight, you're eating too fast, or you're not chewing well enough. You may need to have some saline removed from the band until you can adapt to new eating habits.

For long-term success, we suggest that you avoid soups, chips, cereal, potatoes, ice cream, candy and milkshakes on a daily basis only because these tend to be high in calories and can sabotage your weight-loss efforts. You'll be able to eat them eventually in moderation, just as you'll be able to eat most foods.

We also suggest that you go easy with fruit drinks because they are high in calories and will slide easily past the band. Making sure you get enough high-quality protein will help you keep your energy up.

First-fill blues

You may experience some let-down after your first fill. You may walk out of the office without feeling much restriction and wish that the doctor had made the fill tighter. After all, you've been waiting since surgery for this, and you're eager to get started.

The other possibility is that you feel plenty of restriction at the office, but by later in the day, feel nothing at all. Always keep in mind that this is your first fill. No one, not even you, knows exactly how your stomach is going to react the first time. Your doctor will fill conservatively until he sees how your body responds.

Subsequent fills

The procedure for fills will be the same over the life of your band. Each time, your doctor will discuss how the band has felt, whether you're having any trouble, such as spitting up or difficulty with a food, and how it feels as he adds saline solution to your band.

Each time, you'll also go through the water-sipping ritual afterward. This is necessary because each fill is different.

Just because you were able to sip the water easily on one occasion doesn't mean you'll be able to the next time.

Avoid falling into the trap where you put all the responsibility for weight loss onto your band. People who are constantly trying to fill and unfill their band are trying to make the band 100 percent responsible for their weight loss. This will only slow your progress.

The band, when restricted, depresses your appetite. That's its job.

You should not be hungry if you are eating three meals a day and getting at least 60 grams of protein. If you do depend on your band too much, you can get into a destructive cycle of too much restriction, which leads to maladaptive eating. An example would be to depend on ice cream for your protein because nothing else will go down.

Taking part in an after-care program is a good way to establish good eating habits

Are there circumstances when I might want the band loosened?

Yes. If you become pregnant, one of the benefits of the LAP-BAND® is the ability to remove the saline solution so that you can be assured of providing your baby all the nutrition it needs without compromising your own needs. If you become sick for some reason and your illness requires you to eat more, the band can be loosened. Once you recover and want to continue your weight loss, it can be filled again.

Are there any complications I can get with the port?

In fewer than 1 percent of cases, problems arise with the port.

- *The port may become dislocated. For example, it may turn upside-down into a position that cannot be injected. If this happens, it is necessary to have an operation performed under local anesthesia to reposition it. This is a simple and safe procedure.*

- *Sometimes during a fill, the connecting tube is perforated close to the port. If the tubing is accidentally perforated, it can lead to a loss of saline solution in the band, widening the stomach opening and subjecting you to weight gain. This also can be corrected with a minor operation under local anesthesia. The port is brought to the surface, the part of the tubing that includes the perforation is cut off, and the remaining tube is reattached to the port. The port is then repositioned.*

from the start and head off potential problems. That's because a group of your banded peers can help you decide if what you're feeling is normal or if you're making too many demands on the band.

The good news is that even fills get easier as you learn to listen to your body. Everyone, even long-time bandsters, experiences changes in what they can eat after each fill.

But also, as you become more experienced with the band, it becomes easier to make the appropriate adjustments. Any difficulty or inconvenience is more than offset by the tangible success you experience as the weight comes off. Just ask Tina Johnson, whose story leads off the next chapter.

Tina: From doormat to diva

Before my LAP-BAND® procedure

After my LAP-BAND® procedure

Chapter 8 | Learning to Say Yes to Yourself
(and No to Others)

At her heaviest, Tina Johnson weighed 257 pounds, yet she was only 5-feet-4-inches tall. Tina was one of those people who pour their energies into taking care of others at the expense of themselves. She was embarrassed by her size, she says, and when she went to trade shows or met with clients in her job as an administrative assistant, she would try to cover up how big she was with big clothes. "I really let myself go," she says of her weight gain, and, like so many overweight people, she knew she had to find a solution. The Forney, Texas, resident heard about the LAP-BAND® through a contest on the radio. The surgery was being offered as a prize. And although she didn't win the contest, the experience got her fired up about the procedure. She was banded in December 2004.

One thing that changed almost immediately was the way she cooked for her family. Before banding, "I was thinking that they've got to have a big meal, and I've got to have a big meal," she says. "I grew up with lots of food on the table, and you were expected to clean your plate."

In the process of learning to prepare smaller portions for herself, she encouraged her family to eat smaller portions and healthier food as well. Tina was fortunate to have a supportive family that didn't resist changes spurred by her weight-loss program.

An exercise video also helped Tina say yes to

herself in a new way. "I'm still doing Walk Away the Pounds *in my home with hand weights three times a week," she says. The video series includes several tapes and, depending on which tape she chooses, Tina can vary her distance from one to three miles, walking in place.*

"When you're larger like I was, even though you're starting to lose weight, you don't have the energy to go out and do a bunch of exercising." She adds: "I've had so much fun with it."

Today, Tina is down to 140 pounds, and she no longer worries about going to trade shows or meeting clients. "I go up with a smile on my face and shake their hand," she says, flush with newfound confidence. And she loves some of the unexpected attention that has come her way since losing weight.

Here's one of her favorite stories: She and her husband live in a small town and have known each other most of their lives. "We went to a ballgame," Tina says, "and someone asked my husband when we had divorced." The person could not believe that the woman with him was Tina, although her husband assured the old friend that she was. "Just to hear something like that, it's so exciting," she says.

Tina had a strong marital relationship going into the surgery, which meant she experienced more support than resistance to her weight loss. Even at her heaviest, she says, her husband was devoted.

Still, he loves the change: "When I was so heavy, he'd go to Victoria's Secret, but he'd just buy the lotion. Now he can go in and buy me a negligee. It's so exciting."

As you begin to lose weight with the LAP-BAND®, your life – and the way you think of yourself – will change. We cannot tell you exactly what your experience will be, but we can tell you that people who are banded report big changes on the way to reaching their weight-loss goal.

These changes start with the honeymoon the moment you are banded and continue until the day you finally come to believe that your weight loss is permanent. (If you have been on diets, there will definitely be moments on the LAP-BAND® journey when you wonder: "When is the weight going to come back?" Because it always has before.)

The weight-loss part of your journey might be as short as a year or as long as three or four, even five years. There's no right length of time. But we do find, having

Will I need plastic surgery for the surplus skin after I lose a lot of weight?

This varies with the individual. In any case, plastic surgery is usually not considered for at least a year or two after the initial operation because the skin may mold itself around the new body tissue. It's important to give the skin the time it needs to adjust before considering plastic surgery. That said, some people who lose a lot of weight after LAP-BAND® surgery do feel better about themselves with plastic surgery if the skin does not remold.

taken this journey with so many patients, that it's possible to predict and prepare for some of the things you'll encounter.

In the broadest terms, here's what happens: As your body shrinks, your self-esteem grows, and the more you say yes to yourself, the more you may find yourself saying no to others. During this process, your emotional comfort zone will change, which can challenge the comfort zones of those around you.

Change in any form is scary for most people, even if it's a positive change. You may not like being fat, but you are at least used to it, and you know how others react to you as a fat person.

But even before people can see a visible change in your weight, you'll be venturing outside your comfort zone as you move through the honeymoon-divorce period with your band. The changes at times may feel frustrating and unfamiliar because predictability is part of what makes a comfort zone comfortable.

But there will also be moments along the way when your spirits soar because you have accomplished something you never dreamed possible before becoming banded. In this and the coming chapters, we give you a more detailed road map of some of these changes so that when you

hit your personal speed bumps, you'll have some idea what's going on, what to do, and how to proceed.

And we'll tell you how to make the most out of something we call non-scale victories in Chapter 10 to energize your journey and fuel your determination to put those speed bumps behind you.

Giving up old beliefs & strategies

Let's start by looking at some typical beliefs and strategies that overweight people rely on to make their way in the world. This isn't a comprehensive or scientific list. It's strictly anecdotal, and there are always exceptions. But when we talk about getting outside your comfort zone, we have found that it often involves challenging and changing one or more of these beliefs.

• **Fat people try harder.** A lot of heavy people feel that they're at a disadvantage in the world from the get-go. They believe they must try harder and prove themselves because being fat is a huge deficit, no pun intended.

And let's face it: There's some truth to this. American society does have a fat prejudice, which has been documented many times over. Some fat people take this challenge personally and, to compensate, make it their mission to be the best at everything: the best friend, the best co-worker, the best room mother, the best neighbor.

They feel compelled to throw the best parties. Go to work early and stay late. Take the most work home. Buy the best gifts. Volunteer. Cook the kids dinner while babysitting. Work on a co-worker's project at the expense of their own. In short, they're determined to do whatever it takes to prove that they're not just OK, they're super-OK.

• **Fat people are eager to please.** A variation of trying harder is the desire to please everyone. Pleasing is another way to make up for the perceived disadvantage of being overweight. Often without realizing it, pleasers put everyone else's needs ahead of their own – friends, spouses, children, parents, co-workers, even pets.

Wake them up in the middle of the night with a problem, and they're there for you. Need someone to walk your dog while you're out of town? They'll do it. Need a ride to the airport? They'll rearrange their schedule to make it work. Anything their kids need – help with a science project, a Halloween costume, a ride to soccer practice – they'll make it happen, even when they feel bad, they're tired or it's an inconvenience.

"No" isn't in their vocabulary. That is, until they start losing weight.

• **You can make up for being fat with personality.** Some heavy people try to compensate for their low self-worth by turning on the charm: At some level, they believe that if they're funny, no one will notice their weight. Or it won't matter. Maybe you know someone who's the fat-lady comedian, or the jolly fat man. They make everyone laugh, no matter how they feel inside.

• **You can make up for being fat with brains.** It's the same principle as personality. If they become the go-to brainiac, their fat won't matter. You'll overlook it and like them because they're so smart.

• **Fat people have a right to be angry.** The opposite of the personality king or queen is the sullen, angry fat person. They're pissed off at the world. No one is going to get inside their head.

Their comfort zone is a box with a "do not enter" sign on the door, and most people are happy to oblige.

· **Being fat means being invisible.** Just about every fat person has had the humiliating experience of walking into a roomful of people where no one makes eye contact, no one smiles and no one speaks to them. People may look in your direction, but they act as though you're not there.

Some big people take this rejection to heart and do everything they can to *be* invisible. Being invisible becomes their comfort zone. They deflect attention to others. They make little or no eye contact. Look down. Shuffle around the edges of a crowd. Sit by themselves. Watch from the sidelines. Or, paradoxically, they lock onto eye-contact so you can't see how fat they are. The bigger they get, the more invisible they try to become.

• **Fat people have good excuses for being fat.** Some, at least, find comfort in making excuses to avoid taking action. It's not their fault that they're fat. It's baby weight from when they were pregnant, even though the baby is 20 years old.

Some say to themselves, "Oh, we're just big people." Or, "We're big-boned." Others persistently see themselves as smaller than they are: "I'm not really that big," they say, despite the contrary messages from the mirror and the scale.

Excuses are all forms of denial. And while it's true that there may be extenuating factors that have prevented them from losing weight, these people are not willing to take responsibility for *any part* of their weight gain.

All of these scenarios suggest that somewhere, sometime the fat person has bought into the belief that they're not worth very much. They have low self-esteem. Weight gain can be the cause, the result or both.

People get banded because they've tried so many other weight-loss strategies and failed. Their self-esteem has taken a beating. They really want this to work.

But they fear, deep down, that it won't.

You may not believe it starting out, but the LAP-BAND® will give you the tools you need to succeed not only at losing the weight but keeping it off. And as the pounds begin to drop away, a curious thing happens: In small ways at first, you begin to whisper yes to yourself and no to others.

When you are accepted as a patient to receive the LAP-BAND®, you make a commitment to do your part to make it work. Maybe it doesn't seem like a big commitment at the time, or maybe you are so fed up with being fat that you are sure you'll be able to keep your part of the bargain. But you commit to the lifestyle changes and doing 30 percent of the work. You may think you're making this commitment to your doctor, but it's really a commitment to yourself. Because your doctor won't be there watching 24 hours a day.

You don't really sign on to say no to people. But it will happen, perhaps like this: You find yourself sitting at the table, concentrating on eating slowly and chewing your food well, especially when you're first learning how this works for your body, and other family members are wolfing their food down like always.

They're finished. You're not. They don't understand what's taking you so long. They get annoyed.

Or, you want to go out with your co-workers at lunch, but they're headed for McDonald's, and you're not sure you can get the protein you need from a meal there. You say no because getting at least 20 grams is your new priority, and you won't feel satisfied if you don't. They don't get it; you used to love McDonald's.

Or, perhaps you buy and prepare fish for dinner because it's the easiest protein for you to eat. You do this, even though your family or your roommate complains that you're stinking up the house. You don't really feel like you're saying no. You're just saying yes to fulfilling your commitment to eat 60 grams of protein a day.

Or, maybe you find that drinking 48 ounces of water a day means you have to take additional bathroom breaks at work, and your boss doesn't like it. Or, your commitment to exercise means investing in a pair of good walking shoes when your daughter thinks she should get a new outfit. She wonders when your shoes became so important.

Maybe you get to the point where you're walking an hour every day, and a friend wants you to go to Starbucks for a

Frappuccino. A part of you would love to say yes, but it conflicts with the only time you can walk, and exercise is part of your new lifestyle.

Part of saying yes to yourself is saying no to others. Making the commitment to follow the rules is among the first steps to gaining control of your life. Once you make the commitment, you can't continue to do the same old things in the same old way.

Can you see how this sets off a chain-reaction with other people's comfort zones? Can you see how this will nudge those around you to reshape their comfort zones, too?

In the best of all worlds, your family, friends and co-workers will be supportive, just as Tina's family was. They will accept and embrace the need for everyone to adjust. They will become your cheerleaders, and they'll partner with you on your weight-loss journey.

But sometimes, the people around you aren't prepared for you to change. They will resist your changing. They may even discount or devalue your weight-loss success, because you didn't do it "on your own."

Maybe you've been the employee who always volunteers to work late. Then one day, you don't volunteer because you have plans. Your boss and co-workers don't like this new wrinkle. Now one of them will have to stay instead. They might say, "That's not like you." What they don't see – or don't want to see – is that it is very like the new, emerging you.

Or, perhaps your adult children assume you are their on-call, anytime baby-sitter, and you tell them you can't come on such short notice because if you do, you'll miss your workout. Now they have to get outside their comfort zone and either accommodate you or find another sitter. Saying yes to yourself and no to others may start slowly, but it will gain momentum.

You also may be surprised to find yourself becoming angry when people resist your changing. Feeling angry isn't bad if it means you're starting to stand up for yourself. Anger can actually be a positive change if you've tended to let people walk all over you. But it may be unfamiliar.

At the same time, getting banded is not an excuse to become a rage-aholic. There are constructive and healthy ways to express anger, and feeling anger is just one sign that your comfort zone is shifting. It will continue to shift throughout your LAP-BAND® journey. At some points, in fact, your comfort zone may seem like a moving target.

Body image

As your body changes, you will also find yourself discovering – or rediscovering – the person inside who isn't fat. We've already discussed how this begins in the divorce phase, when you start to confront the importance you've given to food. It will continue until you reach your weight-loss goal and become convinced that the weight will stay off for good.

For many people, their self-image doesn't keep pace with the reality of their changing body. When they look in the mirror, they still see the fat chick or the guy who's not making progress.

Keeping a record of your weight and measurements is one way of helping you to see yourself more realistically. It can also be a source of encouragement as you watch the numbers go down. Make it a point to write these numbers in a log each time you weigh and measure yourself. When the road gets bumpy and your comfort zone feels wobbly, this will at least give you hard data that document your physical changes and remind you why you're doing what you're doing.

You'll also see your weight loss reflected in your wardrobe, even when you're reluctant to accept it. A lot of people, as they lose weight, continue to dress in big, loose clothes with stretchy waists, as through they're still fat. They don't see the slimming-down person yet. For this reason, another instructive activity is to go to a clothing store periodically during your LAP-BAND® journey and try things on.

Just taking an afternoon to do this can help you begin to grasp that you're smaller now, and you can (and should) dress differently. Remember Sylvia Thompson shopping for clothes in Chapter 3? Take a trusted friend with you who can help you sort out what looks good on your changing body and what doesn't.

Sometimes, too, you're lucky enough to find a salesperson who will take the time to help you and be honest about what looks good and what doesn't. They may not state this directly; rather, they may choose their phrasing carefully, saying things like, "That's not your look," "That's not your outfit," or "Let's try a different style."

But this feedback, whether from a friend or a salesperson, can gently nudge your body image into closer alignment with the reality of your changing body as well as help you dress appropriately.

It's also a good idea to take monthly photographs from the front and side with a person whose height and weight are stable. Comparing the pictures month-to-month can provide a visual tool that helps you adjust to your new body image.

Non-scale victories

During your journey, you'll experience wonderful "aha!" moments that send your spirits soaring. They have nothing to do with inches or pounds per se. They're what we call **non-scale victories**. Even more than numbers, they are powerful motivators to keep you going.

Cynthia's non-scale victory

"I used to always bring a special, oversized T-shirt to the hairdresser because I was too large to wear the smocks he provided. Then one day, well into my weight loss, I walked in and decided to try on a smock just for the heck of it.

"I was thrilled to find that it not only fit, but was kind of big on me. The moment I came out of the dressing room, my hairdresser noticed and cheered. Without saying a word, I handed him the oversized T-shirt and said, 'I won't be needing that anymore.'

"He was so proud of me that he took the T-shirt, ripped it to shreds, and used it to wrap hair for other clients. That was a non-scale victory for me: to go to the hair salon and be able to wear a regular smock."

Non-scale victories are moments of personal triumph, when you discover that you can do something you have wanted to do but weren't able to because of your weight. In addition to fitting into a regular smock at the salon, here are some examples from patients:

- *Walking up a flight of stairs without sweating or becoming winded.*
- *Running up a flight of stairs.*
- *Fitting comfortably into a restaurant booth.*
- *Playing with your children or grandchildren instead of just watching them.*
- *Getting through a day (or an hour) without pain.*
- *Wearing high heels without feeling like you're going to break your neck.*
- *Parking at the mall and walking inside without breaking into a sweat.*
- *Fitting comfortably into a stadium seat.*
- *Crossing your legs when you sit down.*
- *Sitting on a chair without the fear of breaking it.*
- *Buying clothes off the regular rack in a clothing store.*

- *Getting to a certain clothing size.*
- *Not having to ask for a seatbelt extension when you fly.*
- *Easily reaching your private parts.*
- *Seeing your toes when you look down.*
- *Touching your toes.*
- *Being checked out by the opposite sex.*
- *Having a boy/girlfriend.*
- *Being able to work under a car without jacking it up.*
- *Eliminating or cutting back on meds (with your doctor's blessing), for conditions such as diabetes or high blood pressure.*
- *Going to an amusement park and fitting on rides.*
- *Riding a bicycle in a group outing.*
- *Having people not recognize you because you've lost so much weight.*
- *Seeing your collarbones.*
- *Being able to feel your hip bones.*
- *Getting up from the floor without help.*
- *Sleeping better.*
- *Maneuvering through tight spaces in a restaurant or store without fear of bumping people or getting stuck.*
- *Standing in long lines without pain.*
- *Having a child notice some aspect of weight loss, with a statement like, "Daddy, those pants are too big for you."*

But you're not just going to just think about what your non-scale victories might be. You're going to write them down. Allow yourself to dream big: Be willing to include milestones you genuinely yearn for, however far-fetched they might seem. Non-scale victories are part of the rewards for saying yes to yourself.

Keep this list with you at all times. It may take you several years to cross all the items off. But in time, you will. If you're a woman, keep the list in your purse. If you're a guy, put it in your glove box or briefcase. Whether you share the contents of the list with others is up to you.

What's important is that it reflect your true desires.

Non-scale victories are important for another reason. You will need them throughout your journey, not only to affirm that you're on the right track but to counterbalance something called sabotage: the conscious and unconscious efforts by you and others to derail your weight-loss regimen. Sandy McCoy, whose story leads off the next chapter, did an excellent job of deflecting sabotage until life threw her a curve ball.

Sandy: Caught by surprise

Before my LAP-BAND® procedure

After my LAP-BAND® procedure

Chapter 9 | How to Beat Sabotage, the Stealth Enemy

Sandy McCoy is a no-nonsense nurse practitioner from Plano, Texas, who was powerfully motivated to lose weight. "I kiddingly told my patients that I was fat, too — a healthy fat," she says. "Then, all of the sudden I developed high blood pressure and high cholesterol. I had to do something." Ironically, she works for two bariatric surgeons and knew a great deal about gastric bypass. "I knew it was a more invasive surgery than I wanted to have done. So I continued to watch what was on the horizon. Then I started hearing about the band."

After doing some research, she says, "I became very motivated. I felt like this was the right tool for me."

It was time: Sandy weighed 289 pounds and was 5-feet-7-inches tall when she got her band in 2003. "I lost 33 pounds the first month," she says. She also approached food in a creative way. "I didn't deprive myself of anything. I would still have my drink of wine, but I'd have one, not three.

"I was a hot fudge sundae person, and I would schedule having a sundae once a month. That would be my dinner. I'd ask for a single dip instead of two, and I'd leave the nuts and whipped cream off. Then, after three or four months, I didn't feel like I needed it anymore."

It took her only three months to get to the point where she no longer needed blood pressure or cholesterol medication. In just a little over two years, she achieved her goal weight of 150 pounds.

A model patient, Sandy seemed impervious to sabotage, until life dealt her an unexpected double jolt: "Two years ago, I lost both of my parents. I did go through a time where I did put on some pounds. I was stress-eating. I wasn't watching portions. I was eating the wrong foods," she says.

Once she got past that roadblock, she shed the pounds that she had gained back. But her tendency to fall into old habits during the time of stress was instructive.

Sandy faced another challenge when an old injury flaired up and was exacerbated by the

Is it OK if I am spitting up at every meal, but still losing weight?

No, it is not. If you are spitting up at every meal, it's time to have a talk with your surgeon. You may be losing weight at the expense of needed nutrition, and you could pay a price with health problems later, if this is the case. Spitting up at every meal can also be a sign of slippage. The other possibility is that you're not listening to your body when it says, "Do not swallow that," or "You are full." Trying to override those clear messages from your body may result in spitting up. It is always better to lose weight slowly, as impatient as you might be to see results.

band. "As a small child, I drank carbolic acid and burned my esophagus," she says. "The doctors said it would cause trouble some day, but I forgot about it," Sandy says.

"A year ago, I started having severe gastritis and esophageal reflux," she says, a direct result of the childhoood injury. For nearly six months, she worked with unfilling and filling the band, gaining back 43 pounds in the process. Finally, her gastroenterologist suggested that the band come out.

But still Sandy refused to let this derail her determination to lose the weight and keep it off. "I knew when the band was out how easily I gained weight. I knew I needed a tool to assist me."

She talked it over with the surgeons she worked with and made the decision to have the sleeve surgery in which a portion of her stomach was removed (see Page 18).

Both the band and the sleeve taught her patience, Sandy says. "There are times with the band that weight loss becomes slower. You have plateaus. But if you stick with it, the weight will come off." With the sleeve, Sandy had to learn some new skills. "You have to work very hard, whichever you choose."

Although Sandy managed to dodge most of the sabotage bullets, in truth sabotage is one of the biggest challenges people face on their LAP-BAND® journey.

Not terrorist-extremist sabotage that seeks to disrupt life in the free world. Rather, this sabotage originates with the little terrorist inside your head and the heads of others who really don't want you to succeed.

"What's up with that?" you might ask. "Shouldn't I want to be a healthy weight? Shouldn't those closest to me want me to be a healthy weight?"

The answer goes back to comfort zones: Push the boundaries of others' too much, and they become uncomfortable enough to push back. Push your personal comfort zone too far too fast – Sandy was jolted out of hers after her parents' deaths – and it can be your own mind that tries to put on the brakes.

At its most fundamental, sabotage is about sowing seeds of doubt. It's anything that casts doubt on your ability to succeed or makes achieving success more difficult.

Sabotage can make you question or stop doing your part of the weight-loss work. Of course, sabotage is not unique to weight loss. People use it every day in subtle and obvious ways to undermine themselves and others.

But a weight-loss journey can be especially susceptible. Your tools for disarming sabotage will be self-awareness and good support, whether from friends, family, co-workers, banded buddies or an after-care group. But before we talk about ways to defuse it, let's look more closely at the two most common forms of sabotage.

Self-sabotage

Periodically throughout your LAP-BAND® journey, you will confront self-sabotage. This springs from the deeply held belief that you don't deserve to be a healthy weight. It's about buying into that message mentioned in the previous chapter concerning your sense of worth.

What does self-sabotage look like? Fundamentally, it comes down to two messages: "I can't do this." Or, "I don't deserve this."

Here are some examples drawn from our patients. The exact words you use may differ, but chances are the situations will have a familiar ring. And remember, self-sabotage rarely happens on a conscious

What if I lose weight too slowly? What can I do?

Keep your eye on the prize. Some people lose weight faster than others. But at the end of two or three years, the results will be the same, whether it came off faster or slower. As long as you are staying in contact with your surgeon and the scale is going south, you are moving in the right direction. Also, get involved with a support group, if you are not already.

level, so part of defeating it may mean boosting your internal listening skills.

• You begin to lose some weight, and someone notices and tells you how good you look. Out of the blue, you decide you haven't had ice cream in six months, so maybe you'll have some now. Or, you choose "for no reason" to consume more liquid calories, which will slow or stop your weight-loss. Or, "something comes up" and you don't make the appointment for your next fill.

Maybe a compliment or some positive remark has pushed you too far outside your comfort zone – others are noticing how you look, a sign that your invisibility has begun to melt away – and you suddenly experience a so-called random thought about something that will undermine your process.

• In a similar vein, you might get to a point on your weight-loss journey where you begin to be more visible and this becomes the time you decide to start testing certain foods: "I haven't had a milkshake in six months. I think I'll have one." "I haven't had a brownie. I think I'll see what happens if I eat one now."

"It's been so long since I've eaten potato chips." Learn to recognize that these are sly ways of sabotaging yourself.

• On the flip side, after you have given in to temptation and eaten sugary foods or ice cream or some other calorie-dense food, you say to yourself, "I've totally ruined this. The band is never going to work for me." One slip-up, and you decide you are doomed to fail, that this is going to end like every other diet. Statements cast in black-and-white, all-or-nothing terms are almost always a sign of self-sabotage.

• You make excuses for not losing weight and not following the rules. Before she was banded, Sandy did this whenever she would tell her patients that she was a healthy fat person.

These are some typical sabotaging excuses: "This isn't working for me." "I ate a Twinkie because it was the only thing I could find at the hospital visitors' room." "It's been a rough couple of months for me and my wife/husband." "I eat more when I feel stressed." "My family won't let me eat the way I need to." "My daughter, who has no weight problem, gets upset when I don't keep chips in the house." Excuses are one of the most common forms of self-sabotage.

• In particular, you make excuses for not exercising: "I lost my job." "I've been working late." "I'm so tired when I get home." "My child/parent/spouse/cat/dog is sick." "My husband and I have been having problems." "It was too cold to walk yesterday. It's too cold outside today." "I have a hard time getting started." "I don't like sweat." Something always seems to come up when it's time to exercise. Or, you plead time constraints: You just don't have time.

• Continuing the exercise theme, you avoid going to the gym or participating in a public activity because you think people will look at how fat you are and judge you. You just can't face them. Your fear may be real, but it's sabotage when you can't seem to come up with another way to work up a sweat.

• You keep wondering when the weight is going to come back, because it always has before. Or, you convince yourself that this isn't going to work. You're going to be the one person in 100,000 for whom the band just doesn't work. The next thought in this sabotage sequence almost always leads to statements about not deserving to be a thin or a healthy weight. They're variations on a theme: "What did I do to deserve being thin?" "I have no right to be a normal weight." "My body isn't meant to be thin." "I'll never lose this weight."

• Other kinds of self-judgment are also forms of sabotage. You think, "I'm losing weight too slowly. I must not be doing it right." Or, "I'm losing weight too quickly. I must not be doing it right." Or, "I've *only* lost 10 pounds this month. So-and-so said she had lost 20 by now. Something must be wrong with me."

When you say such things to yourself and they make you doubt, that's a sure sign of sabotage.

Self-sabotage is all about your interior dialogue. It's the negative things you say about yourself to yourself. Since some of the tactics for neutralizing sabotage are the same whether it comes from others or from inside your own head, we'll take a look at sabotage by others before discussing ways to overcome sabotage.

Sabotage by others

Sabotage by others can be harder to recognize because it's often disguised as something else, such as concern or wanting to do something for you. It is often well-intentioned. But it's just as destructive as self-sabotage in that it casts doubt on your efforts or makes achieving success more difficult.

Underneath, sabotage by others sends the message that they don't want you to change: You're putting too much pressure on their comfort zones. They like you the way you are, or were.

More specifically, they know how to relate to you as someone who is fat; they don't know what to think about you as someone who is losing weight or even becoming thin. In their minds, you've been labeled and slotted as a fat person, and they don't really want to deal with you any other way.

Your losing weight might also force them to look at aspects of themselves they don't want to look at, such as their own inability to lose weight.

Here are some examples of what sabotage by others might sound like:

• Co-workers, family or friends tell you that you're not being yourself. "You're acting (fill in the blank: high-strung, angry, selfish, difficult)." They're telling you that they aren't familiar with the changes in you, and they want you to go back to the way you were (fat) so they can return to their comfort zones.

• Friends start showing up with cakes, cookies or other goodies, saying things like, "I know how much you like this." Your sister starts bringing your favorite rich dessert to family gatherings and gets hurt if you don't try it. Maybe a co-worker you're forced to pass several times a day offers candy from the jar on his desk when you have asked him not to.

These are subtle ways of throwing up roadblocks to your weight loss. Their message to you is: Slow down. You're leaving our comfort zone.

• Someone pays you a compliment, which feels good, then follows up with a question that casts doubt on what you're doing. "You look great, but – how can you get enough vitamin C? "You look great, but – are you losing weight too fast?" On the surface, these are statements that ostensibly show care and concern, and people who say things like this may sincerely believe that's what they're doing. The way you recognize them as sabotage is whether they create doubt.

• Then there are friends or relatives who take it upon themselves to become your personal food police. This is their misguided way of showing support. They want to know, "Can you really eat that?" Or, "Should you really have that?" They might make a remark like, "It sure seems like you're eating a lot." Or, they'll question your food choices: "Are you sure that's on your diet?" The sabotage message of these well-intentioned souls is that you're still not competent to know what or how much you should eat.

• Sometimes, your weight loss will catch a spouse or significant other off-guard. You may suddenly get questions about where you're going, when you're coming home, who you've been out with, what you've been doing. Getting grilled about comings and goings, when they've never mattered before, is a sign that he or she is uncomfortable with, and perhaps jealous of, the new you. It's definitely a sign that a comfort zone has been threatened.

How to defeat sabotage

It is all but given that you will confront sabotage on your weight-loss journey, from yourself and others, intentional or not. How do your combat sabotage? This is one of the skills you must learn for yourself to reach your ultimate weight-loss goal, but it helps to know that so many others have done it before you.

If you're dealing with self-sabotage, part of the challenge is learning to quiet the negative voice inside your head and to develop the part of your mind that can think creatively and nurture your efforts. If it is sabotage by others, it means standing up for yourself, perhaps in ways you never have before.

• Get support. No matter what kind of sabotage you face, it can help to have a band buddy (someone else who's banded) to talk to, or to get into an after-care support group where the members share your experience of being banded. You need to have someone you can talk to who knows what you're going through. There are so many ways bandsters can help each other, and when you think you might be dealing with sabotage, these are the people you can ask: "Does this sound like sabotage to you? Have you ever had to deal with this? How did you get past it?"

• Take one decision at a time. It's helpful to remember that small decisions are the stuff of big changes. Losing weight with the LAP-BAND® is a marathon, not a sprint.

And while it's useful to keep your eye on the long-term goal, you're only required to make the next small decision: "What can I eat now to get 20 grams of protein for lunch? Will I be able to do that if I go out with the gang?" "Shall I walk the stairs between floors today instead of taking the elevator?" If you're hungry, "What can I eat that will satisfy me and not sabotage my weight loss?" "Have I had enough water today?" "What can I do with my hands right now instead of going for food?" Or, when you're tired and need to exercise, "Can I push myself to walk for 20 minutes right now, even though I'm tired?"

• Learn to use anger constructively. Remember Erin Brockovich, the brassy, single mom who discovered an energy giant was making people sick by polluting a town's water supply? Her anger fueled her determination to bring the company to justice in an unlikely David-and-Goliath match, an accomplishment we all got to cheer in the movie version of her story. That kind of anger is powerful and packed with energy.

When we say use it constructively, we mean use it to resist sabotage and other destructive actions. Let it fuel your will to exercise and take up activities that feed your purpose. For instance, during the divorce phase, if you feel angry when you think about the amount of time you have devoted to food, don't beat yourself up. Flip your anger to the positive with a statement like, "Darn it, I *can* walk around the block, and I *will* do it right now."

Anger can also help you stand up to others, especially if you have been an extreme pleaser. This kind of anger is good, not bad. But don't be surprised when it is met with resistance by those whose comfort zone you've just ruffled.

In confronting sabotage, your job is to learn to **(1) recognize it for what it is, (2)** interrupt the sabotaging message or action, and (3) **override or neutralize it with a message or action more consistent with your goal**. It's not easy. It requires patience and vigilance. It requires clear thinking and listening. And it requires getting outside your own comfort zone and living with discomfort as you come to grips with the new, changing you.

Like anything new, developing this ability to neutralize sabotaging messages takes time. And don't be too hard on yourself, which can be just as paralyzing. Everyone, banded or not, has bad days when they don't make the best decisions.

Remember Sandy's observation about patience? Accept that you're going to have some setbacks. For a lot of people, progress takes place with three steps forward and two steps back.

Once again, we're going to turn to examples from patients for some common sabotage situations. (Note: If you get stuck and find your weight-loss efforts seriously undercut by sabotage that you cannot overcome, it's time to consult a counselor.)

The sabotage: You eat ice cream three nights in a row because it tastes so good.
What kind of sabotage is it? Self-sabotage.
The solution: Once you recognize that this undermines your weight-loss effort, give away what's left of the ice cream or pour it down the garbage disposal. Resolve to recommit to the rules. Then do it.

The sabotage: Someone says, "You're losing so much weight. Are you sure you're doing the right thing? Don't you think you might be losing too fast?"
What kind? Sabotage by others.

The solution: In most cases, you can simply thank the speaker for asking and assure them that you are working closely with your doctor. That's all you need to say. If this happens persistently with a close relative or friend, you may wish to have a heart-to-heart talk with them and explain why this doesn't help you.

The sabotage: A friend or co-worker brings you a special cookie or slice of cake.
What kind? Sabotage by others.

The solution: If the item doesn't fit with that day's food choices, respect yourself enough not to eat it. Then tell them, "Thank you for thinking of me. That looks so good. But I'm going to pass for now." If you can't refuse, thank them and tell them you'll take it home rather than eat it right now. You can give the treat to someone who will appreciate it. Or, if it's an office party or a family gathering where someone has cut a piece of cake for you, take it back to your desk or chair, eat a bite or two, move it around on the plate, cover it with your napkin, then discreetly lose some or all of it in the trash. Bandsters become experts at moving food around to look like they've eaten more than they have. And if you think normal-weight people don't do this, just watch them.

The sabotage: It's too cold/hot to walk outside today.
What kind? Self-sabotage.

The solution: It's understandable that one day might not be suited to exercise. But if you continue saying it's too cold/hot the next day and the next, you need to recognize the sabotage for what it is and shift to a more constructive strategy. If it's too cold/hot outside, ask yourself, "What can I do inside my house to get my heart rate up for 20 to 30 minutes?"

This is where creative thinking comes in. Maybe you march in place while you swing your arms for that time period. That may sound silly, but you will work up a sweat. Maybe you walk up and

down stairs. Or maybe you break out an exercise DVD, like Tina's *Walk Away the Pounds* with Leslie Sansone (Good Times Video). Committing to exercise when you never have before can be challenging. But you can do it.

The sabotage: A family member insists on eating snacks in front of you. (After all, it's their house, too.)
What kind? Sabotage by others.

The solution: First, be proactive about taking care of yourself: Always make sure that you are eating enough protein so that you're not starving, and thus easily tempted, if something like this happens. Second, have a heart-to-heart talk about how you both can compromise without undermining your weight-loss efforts. You might ask them to stash the snacks somewhere out of your sight. Or to not eat them in front of you at the times when you feel most vulnerable. One option is to make your own snack, say a piece of lunch meat and cheese rolled up with a little mayonnaise, to fill you up so the temptation is not fueled by your hunger.

The sabotage: You're just too tired to exercise after you get home from (pick one: work, school, a doctor's appointment,

the kids' soccer practice, etc.).
What kind? Self-sabotage.

The solution: Recognize that excuses are sabotage. Commit to doing something active, such as walking, even if it's for just 10 minutes. Then do it. By the time you've done 10 minutes, you might decide to continue a little longer. But even if you don't, give yourself a pat on the back for following through with 10 minutes. The next time you feel too tired, bump it up to 15 minutes. Also, check "A special word about exercise" on Page 110. It might surprise you to learn that a lot of people who exercise regularly really don't like it, either.

The sabotage: A well-meaning friend constantly monitors what you're eating and asks, "Is it OK for you to eat that?" "Are you eating too much?" Or she offers you only healthy foods at her house.
What kind? Sabotage by others.

The solution: Again, one of the most disarming things you can do is thank the person for their concern. This has the effect of letting them know you hear what they're saying and appreciate how much they care about you. Then remind them that you really can eat anything you want, just in smaller quantities, and that you and your doctor have discussed how and what to eat. If they persist, have the heart-to-heart about not wanting to feel watched and singled out. And yes, this may take you out of your comfort zone. But you can do it.

The sabotage: You notice that a family member or friend becomes increasingly agitated around you and pointedly does not mention your weight loss or your progress. Instead, they ignore it.
What kind? Sabotage by others.

The solution: Sometimes you play a role in a group. You are the designated fat person. When your status begins to change, it upsets the order of the group. Maybe someone else who was second-fattest resents becoming the new fat person. It also means they now must take responsibility for their weight. Or, perhaps your being fat has always made you a "safe" friend or co-worker, and now that you're losing weight, you're becoming more of a perceived threat, whether it's competition on the job or competition for attention.

When you are clearly losing weight and gaining confidence, looking at yourself differently and dressing differently, some

A special word about exercise

Here's the dirty little secret you need to know about exercise: A lot of people who do it don't like to do it. People who exercise even when they don't like it have found something to motivate them that exerts more influence than their dislike. Maybe they like looking fit and trim.

Or they feel better and more energetic after exercise, even if they were tired before they started. Health can be a motivator. Or maybe exercise is an outlet for the day's anger and frustration.

Dirty little secret No. 2: There's no easy, formulaic answer to getting started or keeping up an exercise regimen. Sooner or later with exercise, you simply have to suck it up and get on with it. It does help to start slowly, so you're not overwhelmed, and to use the positive energy of the honeymoon phase – or the anger about the divorce – to get yourself up and going.

It helps to take some time to figure out what kind of activity works best for you and your schedule. Or to change activities when you get tired of one. You might walk at first, then decide to move up to something more vigorous.

Try out different kinds of exercise to see what you can do that keeps you relatively happy. Some people ride bikes. Some people hate bike-riding. Some people jog. Some hate jogging. Some work out with Richard Simmons videos, which are terrific when you're just starting. But some people hate Richard Simmons. Some people can't maintain the discipline of exercising at home alone and need a structured setting, such as a class. Some would rather do it at home where no one's watching.

A lot of women join Curves, a workout studio free of mirrors and geared to the beginner. Still others join a gym. Some get into water-aerobics classes. In the course of this experimentation, you'll also discover the best time of day for you to exercise. Some people are morning exercisers, and some are evening exercisers.

Be willing to try a lot of different ways to get your heart rate up. Keep your doctor in the loop, and don't get too hung up on media or articles telling you what you need to do. Just go for discovering what works for you.

Almost everyone who begins and maintains an exercise program learns to make the best of it and commit to doing it, regardless. There's no magic. It's like Nike says: Just do it.

people may not be ready for the way this impacts their comfort zone. With their silence, they are sending the strongest possible signal: Don't change. But by this point, you will have momentum on your side. You won't be willing to go back. If they cannot accept that you're changing, you may have to spend less time with them. If a job is at stake, you may, at the extreme, have to change jobs.

The sabotage: There's not enough time when you get home to exercise and make dinner for the kids, too. Plus, you know you're not getting enough quality time with them.
What kind? Self-sabotage.

The solution: Get your kids involved in your weight loss. Ask them to go for a walk or take a bike ride with you. Let them ride their scooter or skateboard. Push toddlers in a stroller. When you get back to the house, make something that requires a little prep time and ask the kids to help. A child can stir a sauce. Or open a bagged salad and put it in bowls. With just a little imagination, you can create a situation where you're spending quality time with them and setting a good example about exercise and food choices, too.

Preparing for the new you

Each time you successfully neutralize sabotage, you move a step closer to your weight-loss goal. Your confidence grows. Your waistline shrinks. You're well on your way to what might be called the endpoint of your weight-loss journey: accountability. And as Tina Mahan's story shows at the beginning of the next chapter, accountability is, more than anything, accepting responsibility for one decision at a time, one day at a time.

Tina: Accountable from the get-go

Before my LAP-BAND® procedure

After my LAP-BAND® procedure

Chapter 10 | The End Game: Accountability

It took Tina Mahan, a home child-care-provider who lives in McKinney, Texas, nearly a year to get insurance qualification for the LAP-BAND®. Having worked so hard for that made her determined to stay on track. She was also tired of always being tired, and had back and foot problems that required surgery. It was time for a change, and she wasn't about to mess it up. "I said, going into this, 'I'm going to do exactly what they tell me to do. I'm not going to cheat. I want to reach my goal.'" She's lost 82 pounds since she was banded in late 2005. Today she is at her goal weight of 130.

"I had been overweight since the birth of my first child," Tina says. She has three kids now. "I just kept on gaining and gaining. I did Weight Watchers and Metabolic Research [Center]. I went to a gym. I would work out, lose 20 pounds. But I couldn't lose any more. I would get frustrated and give up."

At her heaviest, she weighed 220 pounds; she's 5-feet-1½-inches tall. So when a friend who was a registered nurse told her about the LAP-BAND®, she was ready to consider it.

Being motivated doesn't mean it was easy. The hardest part for her, she says, was not being able to drink while she ate. "All my life I had been drinking while eating. But once the band was in, I couldn't do that." She set her mind to learning how. She knew if others had done it, she could, too. "Now, I can go an hour and a half without getting a drink after I eat."

She has also found creative ways to fit activity into her life, including running with her daughter, who was too young to run alone for her track training. "She runs two miles," Tina says. "The first time, I would stop, relax, walk a couple of steps, then continue. I eventually learned to run without stopping." Now, she and her husband trade off running days with their daughter. They also like to go bowling.

Throughout her journey, Tina says, she kept telling herself over and over that it wasn't *going to work if she didn't do what the doctor told her. Now that she's achieved her goal weight, she has arrived at that place mentally where she believes she can sustain it. During the summer, she took the ultimate step: She and her doctor decided to unfill her band completely. "For me to maintain my weight for that long a period, I know it's not going to come back." Tina adds firmly: "I'm not ever going to gain that back."*

When you think about the end point of your weight-loss journey, accountability is probably not the first word that comes to mind.

Excitement, maybe. Or a sense of accomplishment. But accountability? Yes. It's the foundation for sustaining your target weight for the rest of your life.

Accountability means you must take responsibility for your actions and their consequences. This is what normal, healthy people do. It doesn't mean their lives – or your life – will be problem-free. It does mean that they will have learned to be accountable to themselves, a skill that having the band helps you master.

Remember before you were banded when you might have done something like sneak some ice cream or a candy bar? Once you reach a state of accountability, the idea becomes absurd: How can you sneak something past yourself? The short answer: You can't.

Here's something else you might have done before being banded: avoid the scale when your clothes felt tight. You might have told yourself that gaining weight isn't real if you don't step on the scale. But when you become fully accountable, this kind of ostrich-in-the-sand denial just doesn't work.

Being accountable means that if you eat a piece of cake or some ice cream one

Will I be able to maintain my goal weight, once it's reached? For how long?

As long as you follow the guidelines for eating and activity and stay in touch with your surgeon, you should be able to maintain your weight loss for the rest of your life. Remember, too, that morbid obesity is a chronic disease process and holding it at bay requires lifelong vigilance with good health-care practices.

How does my body know when to stop losing weight?

Once you hit your goal weight, you can work with your surgeon to find an appropriate level of band restriction that allows you to maintain your weight.

day, you take responsibility for lightening up on non-nutritious food the next. It means exercising, even if you hate doing it. It means you get on the scale, weigh and accept, sometimes reluctantly, whatever the scale might say. And if you notice your weight creeping up, it means making an appointment for a fill and keeping it.

Being accountable means fully accepting that you are in the driver's seat: You're the one with your hands on the wheel, and your feet control the gas and brakes. You're in control of your body, what goes into it and how active it is.

You won't always do things perfectly; nobody does. But you take responsibility for your actions. For many fat people, this is a radical change in thinking that the LAP-BAND® journey helps to promote.

During the journey, each time you made a conscious decision to eat your protein or say no to a sugary drink, each time you made time for some kind of activity, each time you found a way to busy your hands without it involving food, you were practicing for the moment when such decisions would form the basis of

your day-to-day living. That's also what following the rules (like going slow and chewing small bites) is all about.

There are two additional signposts that suggest you've completed your weight-loss journey.

Developing patience is one. You may notice that you are more patient: patient with yourself, patient with your body, patient when you stumble, and patient for results.

The other signpost is arriving at the point mentally where you truly believe that the weight isn't coming back. After waiting so long for the other shoe to drop, you finally realize that it isn't going to happen as long as you continue to fulfill your part of the LAP-BAND® commitment.

These characteristics develop slowly over time, and at points, you may say, "Am I there yet?" Generally, our patients tell us, you will know when you have passed these signposts. If you have to ask, you've still probably got a little ways to go.

Relationships

One of the most freeing aspects of weight

What if I'm too ashamed to attend an after-care meeting because I haven't followed the eating guidelines?

When you feel embarrassed and want to hide because you have not eaten like you're supposed to is the perfect time to get involved. A support group will be made up of your strongest allies; you're all on the same journey together. Another approach is to find a banding buddy who can hold you accountable. As buddies, you don't become the food police. Rather, you offer the kinds of supportive statements and encouragement that help to keep one another on track. Your banding buddy can brainstorm ways to help you overcome so-called bad behavior. And your buddy can celebrate the small victories that others might not understand.

loss is the change in how others treat you.

First, you will no longer be invisible. The armoring of fat and the way your weight defined who you were also will have vanished. You will begin – or return to – your life as a normal-size person. This may mean less avoidance by others. You will no longer be ignored, shunned or judged by people who are uncomfortable with bigness.

Your weight will no longer be the first thing a stranger sees or reacts to. The first few times this happens – and it usually happens well into your weight-loss journey but before your goal is reached – can be unsettling. It's one of those changes that challenges your comfort zone. But the more weight you lose and the more often it happens, the more comfortable you will become. Pretty soon, you won't think much about it because it will be your new normal.

Losing a lot of weight is like any other significant life event that requires people to adjust the way they think of you. Your relationships with others will change because something about you has changed.

There would be similar adjustments if you got a divorce, say, or moved to another part of the country because of a job transfer or the pursuit of a new career.

In the case of a divorce, there would be some friends who would remain friends through and after the process, and there would be some you would lose. There might be those who feel more loyal to your ex-spouse, or who might be part of a couple that finds it difficult to build a new relationship with you as a single.

A move to another part of the country would also cause relationships to change. Invariably, there would be friends who would remain friends. But there would probably be some friends with whom you would eventually lose contact.

The nature of the relationship before the life change has some bearing on what will happen after. But it is a certainty that your relationships with others will change, some for better and some for worse, as you make the transition to a slimmer you.

It's to be expected that some friends may not embrace the new you, as we discussed in Chapter 8. They simply may not be willing to adjust their comfort zones as you change.

If you were part of group of overweight friends, for example, your losing weight may stir jealousy or resentment. Some people may silently wait for you to fail so you can go back to being your old (familiar) self. They may dislike that you are starting to develop a life away from them.

Or, if you were a safe friend when you were fat - perhaps you were someone who didn't feel attractive, who only listened and who never talked back - you may become threatening as you become slimmer and more confident. This doesn't mean you're in danger of losing every friend. But we often hear from patients that some people just can't make the transition. It's nobody's fault; your weight loss is just too much change for some to deal with.

But the positive side is that you'll develop new relationships. As you get out more socially, it's natural to meet new people. If you do things with other bandsters, there's already a common bond from which a friendship might grow.

If you take up new activities, such as a hobby that keeps your hands busy or a physical activity like ballroom dancing, you'll do these among people who share your interest. Maybe you decide to start attending church or to take a class. All the new places you go hold the potential for new friendships.

Dating and the opposite sex

Sometime before your reach your goal, members of the opposite sex will begin noticing you. Like so many aspects of the LAP-BAND® journey, this can be exciting and scary at the same time. If you are married or in a committed relationship, you can simply savor the flattery. It's fun. It's uplifting. It's cool to be noticed. Some bandsters even put this on their list of non-scale victories.

But if you are single, and especially if you have been fat most of your life, losing weight and being noticed by the opposite sex can mean awakening to the adolescence you never had.

There may be a wild child in you who decides to come out and play. It doesn't matter that you've always been a sensible person. A part of you that didn't get to have a real adolescence now snaps up the opportunity.

You may decide it's fun to wear revealing clothes, to flirt and be flirted with, to put yourself out there, to see what happens. You may also find yourself on an adolescent roller-coaster of emotions: getting crushes, feeling giddy, taking chances, getting let-down. Like teens when the hormones begin to flow, you may experiment with your emerging sexuality.

There's nothing wrong with this, but we'd offer this cautionary note: Always bring an adult along (in your head) to prevent you from doing things that would endanger you or others. This is a time when you can be quite vulnerable to flattery, for example. But not every guy

(or gal) who tells you he loves you really means it; it can be a line to get you into bed. And someone who encourages you to drink a lot may just be trying to break down your inhibitions.

But what if you feel eager and ready for some experimentation? Our advice: Do your homework on sexually transmitted diseases and contraception so that you aren't just running on raw sexual energy. You don't want to dampen your social debut with a mistake, like a sexually transmitted disease, that will be with you the rest of your life.

That said, if you're single and banded, you'll probably start dating at some point. You'll face the same challenges as other singles – where and how to meet people, what to say, how to tell if someone's interested, what to do if they are and you're not, or you are and they're not – but with a few special considerations.

First, having a fat body in your past can make you especially vulnerable to rejection. It can also be tough if someone rejects you because you were fat and they fear that you'll get fat again.

But rejection is part of the dating game for everyone. You'll eventually be glad to deal with the rejection sooner, when your emotional investment is limited, rather than later: After all, if having been fat or someone's fear of your being fat again is a deal-breaker, they're probably not relationship material to begin with. But learning to overcome rejection takes time and practice.

One of bandsters' biggest dating concerns is, not surprisingly, about eating. What happens if you make a date to go out to dinner or lunch? How will you explain how little you eat? What if you're too anxious or excited to eat at all?

Usually, you'll be able to eat something. Although, if for some reason you really can't, give a polite, noncommittal reason: *My stomach is upset. I wasn't as hungry as I thought I'd be. I think I'll just have some iced tea/a cup of coffee.*

You don't have to explain on the first date that you're banded. If you can eat, order as you normally would, and if your date appears puzzled by the small amount of food, say matter-of-factly that you don't eat a lot. That's the truth. You don't have to elaborate. It's also true that some unbanded women deliberately order very little on a first date; they think it's attractive to eat like a bird.

One strategy, if you're feeling uncomfortable, is to get the spotlight off you and onto your date: Ask them questions about themselves. Once they get talking, they're likely to not notice how little or what you're eating. In many ways, the answer to dating qualms is the same for everyone: Just do it, experience it, and decide over time what works for you.

The truth is, you'll go on a lot of first dates. It's the nature of dating, whether you're banded or not. It's true whether you're looking for that someone special or just a pal to have a good time with.

And awkward moments are universal, whether you find these first dates through a dating service, the Internet, church groups, singles groups or friends. One that's common to all singles is letting someone know that you *don't* think there's a connection.

Sometimes, it's easy, especially if you don't think they feel a connection, either. You can acknowledge the lack of sparks and wish them luck on their journey. But what if you feel a connection and they don't? Remind yourself that the relationship won't be what you're looking for if they're not on the same wavelength.

Conversely, if someone likes you but you're not interested, tell them in a kind way that it doesn't feel right for you, then add that you'd like to keep their name and number in case you run into someone you think they might like. It allows them to save face. And who knows? You might run into someone you think is perfect for them.

The other unique dating issue that comes up for bandsters is this: When, in a budding relationship, do you tell someone you're banded? That depends. Honesty is always the best policy with someone who might become significant in your life. But choosing the right moment can be challenging.

In the best of circumstances, the topic and the time to discuss it are going to come naturally in conversation as your relationship develops. Just make sure to bring it up before you decide to become intimate. And, again, if the band is a deal-breaker, it's better to find out sooner than later and move on down the road.

Like the LAP-BAND® journey, dating is a process that requires persistence and courage – and that goes for anyone. Lots of people not only survive it, they have fun and meet interesting and exciting people along the way. Lots find that special, committed relationship, too.

How spouses adjust

When one spouse gets banded, we like to say both spouses do. That's because a person in an intimate relationship cannot escape the changes going on with his or her mate. Put another way: A spouse can't insulate himself or herself from the LAP-BAND® journey in such close quarters. If the marriage is good, sharing the LAP-BAND® experience will likely make it stronger. You develop a deeper, richer relationship because of taking the journey together. But if a marriage is wobbly to begin with, the band has the potential to weaken it further.

A relationship can't continue with one spouse going one direction and the other spouse going in another. Sooner or later, something's got to give.

Here's an example of how this might happen: Say you are fat and don't feel very good about yourself. You may be grateful just to have a spouse, someone to love you just the way you are. You may have shown that gratitude by always putting your spouse first or making your spouse's needs the focus of your life. But when you start losing weight and feeling better about yourself, you're not quite so grateful. You're not quite so willing to drop everything to make them happy.

If your spouse happens to prefer things the way they were, he or she isn't going to like it when your priorities shift. He or she will resist change. Another possibility is that, as you lose weight, you become more attractive and assertive. This makes some spouses jealous or insecure. The old you may have been fat, but your spouse didn't worry about losing you.

When one person changes and the other resists, it's a recipe for trouble. At some point, an ambivalent spouse with a banded partner usually faces a choice: Either become more involved and supportive, or risk being left behind. This is one reason we encourage spouses to participate in our after-care program. Besides the benefit it provides to bandsters, an after-care program gives banded spouses a chance to hear what other couples are going through and how the band impacts their lives together.

The importance of using an after-care program

Not everyone has access to an after-care program. But if you do, take advantage of it. It's an opportunity to get back in the social swing as well as share and swap stories and information. Here's how the after-care program works in Dr. Jayaseelan's practice: We offer a range of activities, from regular meetings to special outings throughout the year. We announce these in our newsletter.

Typically, we schedule four outings every month. You might attend one or all four. The office sets up the location and, if it's a restaurant, makes the reservation; everyone is responsible for paying for their own meal. Spouses and others are encouraged to attend.

The dinners provide an informal setting without a doctor present where banded people can talk about what they're going through. They can compare their experiences with that of others. It's also an opportunity for people who aren't banded to ask questions and talk with people who are.

We also encourage people to attend no matter where they are on the journey because they might learn something new or provide insight for someone else. There will always be people who are ahead of you and behind you.

We also hold monthly meetings with the doctor present. This is a chance to get in front of your surgeon in a social situation and ask questions.

At the beginning, we'll go around the room and people will introduce themselves, reporting how much weight they've lost and how long they've been banded. We might bring in a dietitian, a counselor or a plastic surgeon to talk about a specific topic.

At one of our most successful meetings, we spent the whole time tasting protein drinks because people had complained that they were having trouble finding one they liked. (For the results of our tasting, see "Protein drink taste test" on Page 124.)

We also arrange other outings and activities. These include field trips to local clothing stores to try on clothes and see what looks and feels good as people's bodies start changing. We sometimes set up outdoor walks. Another activity that's well attended is our **swaps**. We do these two or three times a year. We encourage people who are losing weight to bring clothes that are too big and swap for stuff that fits. Whatever is left over gets donated to a charity. All of these outings, dinners and meetings provide a safe place for banded people to take some risks and practice venturing outside their comfort zones.

End game: a healthy life

When you reach your target weight, when you accept that the weight isn't coming back, and when you have achieved accountability in your day-to-day life, you will have reached the end game of the LAP-BAND® journey: a healthy life. What does that mean? It means your life

Rules for Dating

Here's a common-sense strategy for anyone who's starting to date, especially if you're working through a service or the Internet, where you don't know the person.

• When you agree to meet a new person the first time, make it a public place, preferably during the day or early evening.

• Make sure someone – a friend or family member – knows where you're going and when. Give them any information you have about your date, such as name, phone number, even a picture.

• Limit yourself to two drinks. And if you want to be extra-cautious: Don't drink anything that someone else orders for you while you're away from the table.

• Agree to call your friend or family member once you get home from the date, no matter what time it is.

no longer revolves around your weight. Instead, you have the time and energy to devote to thoughts and activities of everyday living.

This represents a quantum leap for the grossly overweight. When you are fat, so much of your time is consumed with adjusting to being fat in a normal-size world that you forget what normalcy is.

When you are fat, you wake up in the morning dreading how much your feet are going to hurt when you put weight on them for the first time of the day. You worry about hygiene issues. You don't want to look in the mirror. You worry about things like whether you're going to sweat through your clothes. You may look at a chair and wonder if it will break when you sit on it.

When you are fat, you are constantly scanning your surroundings without even thinking about it for potentially awkward situations: *What's the easiest way to get to the restroom without bumping into someone? Where's a booth I can fit in? Will I be able to turn around in the restroom stall? Are those people watching me while I eat? Will that salesperson ask to help me or just scowl?* So much inner dialogue is about being fat and how to get through the day without being embarrassed or uncomfortable.

Living normally gives you back a lot of your brain. When you wake up in the morning, you think, "Here I go again!" You pop out of bed. It doesn't occur to you to think about pain. You have energy. Showering's a breeze. You have a closet full of clothes – options like you never had when you were fat. You like the person you see in the mirror. You slide easily behind the wheel of a car. And when you walk into a mall, you have the whole mall to shop, not just the one store for big people.

You feel good about yourself. And your inner dialogue isn't about getting through the day fat. It's about things like your spouse, walking the dog, what the kids need for school, whether you're late for work, what to fix for dinner, when you'll work out.

This isn't just a matter of trading one set of concerns for another. When you finally get the weight off your body, the bonus is the weight you take off your mind. It really is like that old cliché: You don't realize how much your head hurt till you stop hitting it with a hammer.

You have no idea how free your mind and body can be when fat stops controlling your life. And thanks to the LAP-BAND®, you never have to go back to being fat, or thinking fat, again.

Protein drink taste test

Because there are so many protein drinks available, we taste-tested several at one of our after-care group meetings. We didn't actually rank them, because people had strong preferences about shake vs. nonshake texture. But we have included comments and what people liked or didn't like about them. All are available online, if you don't live near a big city. Here's a rundown of our results:

Labrada Lean Body Hi-Protein Milk Shake: The overall group favorite. Tastes best cold. Each 17-ounce/500mL serving has 40 grams protein, 9 grams fat (1 sat fat), and 5 grams fiber. Flavors: Vanilla Ice Cream, Chocolate Ice Cream, Bananas & Cream.
Web site: www.labrada.com

IDS New Whey '42' Liquid Protein: Sweet, but easy to drink in 3.1-ounce shots. Contains 42 grams protein. Flavors: Fruit Punch, Grape and Orange. (Grape was the favorite.) IDS also makes New Whey '25' Liquid Protein, which comes in 2.9-ounce shots and contains 25 grams of protein. Flavors: Fruit Punch, Blue Raspberry.
Web site: www.idssports.com

EAS Myoplex Original Ready-to-Drink Shakes: This was Dr. J's favorite, especially the Chocolate and Vanilla flavors. Each 17-ounce/500 mL serving contains 40 grams protein, 7 grams fat (1 sat fat), 6 grams fiber. Flavors: Chocolate, Vanilla, Cookies & Cream, Mocha, Rich Dark Chocolate, Strawberry.
Web site: www.eas.com

Atkins Advantage Shakes: OK and easy when you're on the go, plus they're widely available at big-city grocery stores. Each 11-ounce/325mL serving contains 15 grams of protein and between 2 and 4 grams of fiber, depending on the flavor. Flavors: Chocolate Delight, Strawberry Supreme, Creamy Vanilla and Chocolate Royale.
Web site: www.atkins.com

Nature's Best Zero-Carb Isopure: Good if you don't want the shake taste and texture. Comes in Kool-Aid-type flavors. Tastes best cold. A 20-ounce/591mL serving contains 40 grams of whey protein. Flavors: Passion Fruit, Pineapple Orange Banana, Mango Peach, Alpine Punch, Icy Orange, Grape Frost, Apple Melon, Blue Raspberry.
Web site: www.naturesbest.com

Nature's Best Zero-Carb Isopure Powder: Tastes better if you mix it with skim milk, but it's OK with water. Dutch Chocolate was the favorite. The Creamy Vanilla's pretty good, too, if you mix with fruit. Each scoop contains 25 grams of protein.

Flavors: Strawberries & Cream, Dutch Chocolate, Creamy Vanilla, Pineapple Orange Banana, Mango Peach, Cookies & Cream, Alpine Punch, Apple Melon.
Web site: www.naturesbest.com

Just for fun: Protein bars taste test

We also taste-tested protein bars, and these were the winners. It's important to note that we treat these as meal replacements, not snack bars, because of the higher fat and saturated fat content.

ISS Research Oh Yeah! Protein Wafer Bars: Peanut Butter Cup was the favorite flavor. These are wafer sticks with cream filling and come two to a serving. Each serving contains 14 grams protein, 13 grams of fat (6 sat fat) and 2 grams of fiber. Other flavors include Vanilla Toffee Fudge, Creamy Vanilla & Caramel, Chocolate Chocolate, Chocolate Peanut Butter, Chocolate Mint, Vanilla Crème, Vanilla Peanut Butter Crème.
Web site: www.issresearch.com

BioNutritional Research Group Power Crunch Bars: These crisp wafers filled with protein "crème" were crowd-pleasers, especially the Cookies & Crème, Wild Berry Crème and Peanut Butter Crème. Each cookie contains 14 grams of protein, 12 grams of fat (5 sat fat) and 1 gram fiber. Other flavors: Cinnamon Bun, Peanut Butter Fudge, French Vanilla Crème, Triple Chocolate.
Web site: www.bnrg.com

Lost and Found

A Guide to the LAP-BAND® Journey

Index

Numbers in **bold** indicate pages with illustrations or photographs

a